Akashic Records

Understanding Your Soul's History and How to Read It

(A Comprehensive and Introductory Guide to Easily Access the Akashic Records for Yourself)

Daniel Franks

Published By **Tyson Maxwell**

Daniel Franks

Akashic Records: Understanding Your Soul's History and How to Read It (A Comprehensive and Introductory Guide to Easily Access the Akashic Records for Yourself)

ISBN 978-1-998901-53-1

No part of this guidebook shall be reproduced in any form without permission in writing from the publisher except in the case of brief quotations embodied in critical articles or reviews.

Legal & Disclaimer

The information contained in this ebook is not designed to replace or take the place of any form of medicine or professional medical advice. The information in this ebook has been provided for educational & entertainment purposes only.

The information contained in this book has been compiled from sources deemed reliable, and it is accurate to the best of the Author's knowledge; however, the Author cannot guarantee its accuracy and validity and cannot be held liable for any errors or omissions. Changes are periodically made to this book. You must consult your doctor or get professional medical advice before using any of the suggested remedies, techniques, or information in this book.

Table Of Contents

Chapter 1: Understanding Trance States

To comprehend trance states, we must consider the brainwaves' nature. Neuroscientists are able to accurately determine and categorize the frequencies produced by the electrical brain activity using devices known as an EEG. The diverse frequency ranges and visible patterns, like the ones below, represent different levels of consciousness and behavioral patterns.

EXPLORING BRAINWAVES

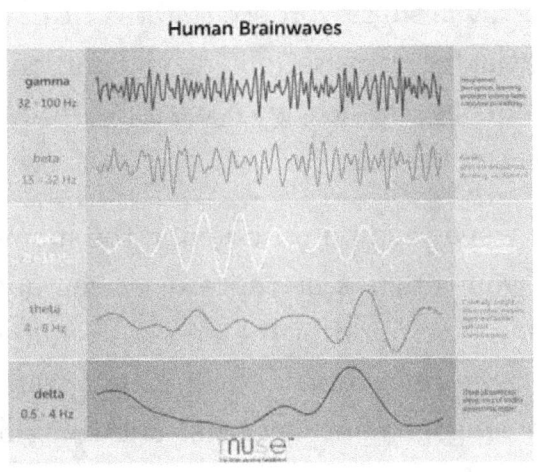

In our training, we focus mostly upon alpha and theta and gamma state. Theta and alpha states are easily induced and we can induce ourselves (or other people) to these state with methods that are prescribed. Gamma states, however tend to be developed by practice, not induced.

As previously mentioned the alpha waves occur when we're in a state of relaxation, yet alert and aware of the world around us. If we're daydreaming, contemplating in contemplation, or in the midst of psychoactive substances, we're experiencing alpha awareness. These states can be beneficial for visualisation and exploration the Astral Spaces, which we'll examine in depth during this Lesson.

Theta waves can be observed in the moment when your brain is at peace or asleep and is sleeping. The mind of the ego has entered a state deep relaxation , but it is in a state of active engagement by the sub-conscious.

2

Theta-induced states are beneficial in deep healing and journey work, since the astral realm is completely involved, and your physical body will be at peace.

Gamma waves can be found when there is a clear concentration and peaceful relaxation when compassion for others is felt as an experience of being. Heart-centered Awareness is the foundation for the Akashic Trancework method, which is why Gamma states are naturally active and developed by integrating the concepts discussed in this handbook.

Delta and Beta states are equally important. Beta waves are found in our states of alertness while delta states are found when we are at our least inert. Both of these states are specifically beneficial for Trancework however beta waves are beneficial for grounding, and delta waves are also present when we have been in deep state of healing. There is no discussion of techniques to stimulate more delta or beta waves within this guide, however there are many methods to accomplish this, including Binaural Beats and breathing exercises.

We encourage you to study the study of the relationship between frequency, sound and brainwave activity more in depth as you're inspired. This understanding serves to explore the complexities of various states of consciousness and also to understand how we easily switch between these states with ease. Let's look more deeply at each of them now.

ALPHA TRANCE

We're involved with astral as well as physical awareness. We're awake and alert however, we're also fully connected and absorbed in our own inner world, our Astral Space. The most sensitive, creative, and creative people enter Alpha Trance all the time. Perhaps we've been called or dreamy or even told that we have a limited attention span. This is mainly due to our society doesn't make the space for those who are naturally Alpha Trancers and also due to the fact that natural

Alpha Trancers are usually able to improve their grounding (see Lesson 0) and to develop more efficient Astral Boundaries (see Lesson 9).

A majority of the visualization exercises that are included in this class can be performed effortlessly and effectively in Alpha Trance. This state can be thought of as to be a kind of "gateway" into Astral Space. Once we have a visualisation of something it is a sign that we are in Astral Space via Alpha Trance. Tranceworkers can also experience Alpha Trance when guiding others through Trancework Journeys (see lesson 27).).

THE ALPHA SPECTRUM

Being aware of the subtle gradations in Alpha Trance can be helpful in guiding others. The differences may be subtle however, careful observation and practice can help you "read" the nature of any trance experience for yourself or those around you.

A Light Alpha Trance is characterized by the active involvement in both physical as well as Astral Space. It is the state we achieve when we are truly enjoying the work we're doing. It's typically a comfortable and relaxed feeling.

Deep A deep Trance is more calm and doesn't require interactions or interaction of any kind. It's the state you experience when you do a little meditation or breathwork in which we are relaxed, but conscious of our body and surroundings. You can be extremely expressive during this state and it is possible to slide into and out of deeper states of theta as we are comfortable with it.

THETA TRANCE

The state of the mind is often thought of as the bridge or the interface to direct contact between the mind's subconscious. In a state of deep theta like a dream, we're so absorbed in the archetypal, inner world that we tend to ignore the world around us completely and interpret everything with an unattached observer perspective we call our Higher Self awareness (see the lesson 10).

One of the main differences that is significant between Theta Trance and normal dreaming However, the key difference is lucidity. It is not surprising that Trancework journeys are often described as lucid dreaming. This understanding allows us to use the power of the imagination to utilize our experiences in the astral realms consciously for healing , and other tasks.

THE THETA SPECTRUM

A mild Theta Trance is characterized by complete involvement in Astral Space and slightly suppressed awareness of physical sensations. While in the state of light, we can be mostly aware of the Astral Space, but our self-protection remains intact although they're a bit more relaxed than when we are in Alpha Trance. It is possible to directly connect with the Higher Self and experience the deep abstractions of Akashic Knowledge here.

If we're deep in Theta Trance the mind is physically and astrally active, while our bodily awareness becomes drastically diminished. We can experience old memories from our lives, enter higher dimensions, connect with our MERKABA (see Lesson 22) or activate the Kundalini or whatever else that the imagination of our creative selves leads us to feel. In this state, work must be balanced by ample groundedness (see Leçon 0).

The process of inducing Theta Trance is usually thought of as difficult, however this is not the reality. The sensation of resting and letting your mind wander around without sleeping or falling into a deep mindfulness, and feeling comfortable and warm as we drift into dreams are some examples of how we are able to enter theta state each day. The tough part in Theta Trance is staying there.

A self-inducing Trance can usually be so deeply at peace that we will are able to fall asleep. This isn't necessarily an issue, as there are times when we require those more profound state of delta to recover or to relax, but when we go into a Trance, we'd like to return something to the experience. This Handbook provides ways of being able to access and sustain certain trance states, so that they can serve the purpose of bringing down our astral experiences into the physical realm . . . Instead of sleeping and forgetting what took place. This is the way you can "read" instead of falling asleep and forgetting everything that happened. Akashic Record by dipping into the deepest recesses of our unconscious mind and returning some important information.

EXPERIENCING TRANCE AT WILL

As the lessons advance, we'll be introducing three different methods by which trance states can be inducible breathwork (Lesson 4) as well as Voice Toning (Lesson 5,) vocal induction (Lesson 6.).

Numerous other techniques exist for deliberately triggering Trance states. The majority of Tranceworkers discover that with just a few hours of practice, they can slide into a variety of states of trance at any time, only by deciding to do it. The most frequently used phrase among practitioners of hypnosis is "all hypnosis' is self-hypnosis'. This is a very powerful statement that we can choose the kind of state of mind we would like to live in each moment. The ability to master specific techniques and techniques will allow us to quickly and effortlessly use the states of mind for specific reasons.

WHY TRANCEWORK?

Toning, breathwork and vocal trance initiation are well-studied and time-tested practices which can be taught by studying a myriad of courses and books. The goal of this site is not to give a thorough analysis of any one of these topics. What differentiates Akashic Trancework and the multitude of other Trancework models is in the way we approach one fundamental issue that once we've entered into the state of Trance how is the next step?

The answer to this question is found in the simple process we refer to as "intentional usage of Astral Space". We've all done it at time or another in our lives. Whenever we think of something, get an image, think of an idea, imagine and daydream or simply remember something, we are deliberately engaging with in our Astral Space.

These are more then "just the imagination". We will show throughout these Lessons the actions we take during these states is important. When we are able to make use of our imagination to connect with our subconscious mind, it opens an avenue to greater levels of consciousness that we'll explore in the following Lesson.

TRANCEWORK SCRIPT 01: EXPERIENCING TRANCE STATES

INSTRUCTIONS:

In this session you'll enter the trance of your own. It can be difficult initially but as these lessons get more advanced, you'll be more adept at controlling yourself through various states of consciousness. Do this exercise and observe how it works, and how you to develop your own methods of self-induction. You might be interested in purchasing the optional Guided Journey Bundle that can help you improve your experience and enhance your integration.

We suggest that you take a recording of yourself speaking the scripts aloud or utilize them as a base for your own exercise. If you are able to find a person who is willing to help, make sure to share your level of experience.

SCRIPT

The first step is to find a comfortable and comfortable place to sit.

Get rid of any distractions. Find a space which is private, secure and comfortable.

At present, you are able to sit on a stool, stand or lie down as you would like. Your eyes can be open or shut. Be sure to be nice and relaxed.

Spend a few minutes to take a deep breath into your lung. Let your stomach expand, fully breathing into your lungs, relaxing gently, without effort.

Now is the time to envision some thing. Something you love or are passionate about, something you like and will make you feel happy or makes you feel content at peace, content and grounded. It could be a favourite restaurant, a spot you enjoy going to or a person you love to spend time with.

Simple is best. Relax and let your imagination run wild without needing to make. It's just a daydream or fantasy and playing with your imagination for an instant like you used to do as a child.

You've entered into a state of Alpha Trance. Let yourself be awestruck by the thing you love to contemplate however it feels most natural for you. It doesn't need to be a visual one. It could be a sensation an sound, the smell. Be open to the experience without judgment.

When you continue to concentrate on this object in your mind You will notice that you are getting more comfortable sitting. It is possible to choose to sit down, obtaining an appropriate back and neck support, or lay down if it's suitable for you. You can be able to keep your eyes open or closed depending on your preference. Be sure you feel comfortable and relaxed while you concentrate on the object that is in your head. Don't be concerned about that object shifting or moving or being replaced with another thing. It's just something to explore.

Connect more and more with this object today. Close your eyes to let you fall into a state of light. You are conscious of your body as well as everything else that surrounds you, but your focus is now inward to yourself, in the space of your Astral Space.

Now, allow yourself to be a part of this subject even more. Allow any you think, imagine or feelings, ideas, or concepts that come up naturally within your brain. Let them drift through the air, keeping only the one thing in your head. Everything else is just flowing by as your conscious awareness disappears.

You are now in the deep state of Trance.

Here, you are able to engage the experience completely. Take in the object for what it really is. Make it look nice. Enjoy it. Taste it. You will love it. You can do whatever you want to do with it in this astral, deep theta awareness.

Relax for a few more breaths and let go of the need concentrate at the thing. Simply let it dissolve in Astral Space. It is possible to recreate this image any time. However, now is the time to let yourself completely relax your body.

Take some more deep breaths, and allow your mind to go away from any desire to perform anything, to imagine any thing, or to imagine things. Relax back into the place of no thought, without concept and play with pure sensation.

Then, allow you to sink further into your own. Relax in the most comfortable place you could possibly find from within and outside. Let your breathing become thick, deep and steady, breathe deeply into this peaceful state.

Take a moment to relax in a state of complete sleep. Let yourself go to sleep if you're needed to, or just take an hour of relaxation. Once you're at your best to wake up, do so by allowing yourself to relax by stretching, breathing and allow yourself time to process these new practices before you move forward with the rest you're doing in the next.

Chapter 2: Awareness

We spend the majority of our lives consciously. This is the way it is since we can't really know every moment that we've experienced on an unconscious level or even be able to comprehend the huge quantity of sensory information that we experience at any moment. Your subconscious as well as its diverse components have developed brilliantly over billions of years , allowing it to take on the bulk of the lifting so that our conscious mind can perform what it excels at and that is focus.

The subconscious acts as an important gatekeeper. It decides which information is important to be kept and what information can be stored away or discarded. The way the subconscious mind process this information to deliver it for the brain's conscious part is mostly controlled by conditioning.

If we're well-nourished and nurtured, information is efficiently processed sorting out and sending the information that the mind requires to live and, if there's sufficient energy left to flourish, it will. "Unnecessary" information is removed and is stored away.

When someone is exposed to traumatizing, damaging experiences The subconscious filtering into a defensive perspective of fear. The brain is equipped to anticipate and shield the person from dangers. The conscious mind starts to focus on the smallest possibility of a dangerous event, releasing enormous amounts of energy in order to defend itself against any threat that is perceived. This type of "fear conditioning" that we consider to be the root of all fear is the cause of the most of the suffering and violence both in the world and within our own hearts.

BENEATH THE SURFACE, BEYOND THE MEMBRANE

To comprehend how crucial consciousness is essential to our existence as human beings, it is necessary to look beyond the boundaries of conventional thinking to gain an understanding of the multidimensional reality. From this angle we are able to see that we aren't in reality only what we perceive, more so, it's the process of perception which makes things "real" regardless of moment, as demonstrated in the well-known "double cut" experiment. The implications are obvious: there exists an enormous array of sensory experience that is outside our senses that are somehow "real" but "not true" in the traditional sense.

This grey, fuzzy region is easily understood in the mathematical concepts of darkness and energy which show just 5% the matter in the universe is accessible to any instrument that humans can imagine. The relationship between dark matter/energy as well as the subconscious mind is simple to draw. The subconscious mind is mostly invisible however, we are guided by it. Dark matter and energy are indistinct however, they exist and determine the limits that define our lives. To comprehend any aspect of the vast, mysterious mysteries in the Universe, it is necessary to first comprehend the most obscure aspects of ourselves.

In Trancework The lines between the realms of reality, unconscious experience spirituality, science, and reality can blur and it is easy to get confused. Consider this statement in mind when looking into other dimensions: If you believe that something is real, it is real to you and has the same power as the real thing that is.

If we are able to be convinced that reality is multi-dimensional, then we are able to change the way we think about our lives. We are no longer creatures, weak, and suffering moving around in an unfathomable ball of mud being a victim of circumstance. Instead we are empowered, immortal, brilliant beings who are here to live life, thrive, and relish the life we live. We can achieve this by activating our higher senses, and can see for ourselves the vastness of our experiences beyond the physical. We can use the awareness we gain to strengthen and nourish our own bodies and those around us.

MULTIDIMENSIONAL AWARENESS

The Dr. Abd'el Hakim Awyan (1926-2008) was a wise-keeper of the Ancient Egyptian Mysteries who often mentioned the fact that the ancient Khemitic people had 360 senses. We don't have a word for the majority of these senses in our contemporary worldview as well as the implications for this assertion are intriguing. What could our understanding of ourselves increase If we were capable of observing through 360 senses? Awyan isn't able to provide specifics regarding the Khemitic senses as the largest study we've come across on this subject only mentions 53 senses, as illustrated below. It is important to note that these senses aren't only restricted to humans however, they are accessible on a certain scale to all living beings.

The Fifty Three Natural Webstring Senses and Sensitivities

From: Ecopsychology in Action

The Radiation Senses

1. The sense of sight and light and sight, which includes Polarized light.

2. The sense of seeing without eyes like heliotropism and the sense that plants have of sun.

3. Color sense.

4. The sense of moods and identities associated with the colors.

5. A sense of awareness of one's visibility, or invisibility , and the consequent concealing.

6. Sensitivity to radiation other that visible light such as radio waves, X-rays, etc.

7. Sensing Temperature and temperature variation.

8. The sense of the season, including the ability to protect, hibernate, and fall asleep in winter.

9. Electromagnetic sense and polarity that is able to produce electricity (as in the brain and nervous system waves) and other forms of energy.

The Feeling Senses

10. Hearing, including resonance as well as sonar, vibrations as well as ultrasonic frequency.

11. The awareness of pressure, specifically under water, underground as well as to air and wind.

12. The sensitivity to gravity.

13. The feeling of excreta for removal of waste and protection against enemies.

14. Be sensitive, especially when you touch the skin.

15. The sense of gravity, weight and balance.

16. The sense of proximity or space.

17. Coriolus sense or the ability to sense the impacts of the rotation of Earth.

18. Sensation of movement. The body's movement and sensations, as well as the sensation of mobility.

The Chemical Senses

19. It's a smell that goes over the nostril.

20. Taste and taste beyond the tongue.

21. Hunger or appetite for food air, water, and food.

22. Hunting, killing, or seeking desires.

23. The sense of humidity, including the sense of thirst, evaporation control, and the ability to locate water or avoid flooding.

24. Hormonal sense as a result of Pheromones and chemical stimuli.

The Mental Senses

25. Internal and external pain.

26. Spiritual or mental distress.

27. A sense of terror, dread of death, injury or attack.

(25-27 are the best places to look for more natural wonders to promote and enhance well-being.)

28. Procreative urges include sexual awareness, courting, paternity, love, mating and the process of raising young.

29. A sense of fun, sport enjoyment, humor, and laughter.

30. The sense of physical location Navigation senses, including an in-depth awareness of the seascapes and land and the position of the moon, sun and the stars.

31. A sense of rhythm and time.

32. Sensing electromagnetic fields.

33. The sense of weather fluctuations.

34. A sense of emotional connection and belonging, community as well as trust, support and gratitude.

35. Self-esteem, including friendship, companionship, as well as the power.

36. Domineering as well as territorial sense.

37. The sense of colonization includes compassion and a receptive understanding of others, at times in the sense of being integrated into the superorganism.

38. The sense of horticulture and the ability to cultivate crops is the case with ants that produce fungus, by algae-producing fungus, or birds who leave food in order to attract their prey.

39. The sense of language and articulation, used to communicate emotions and communicate information in every medium , from the bees' dance to literature.

40. Appreciation, humility and ethics.

41. Form and design senses.

42. Reasoning, which includes memory and the ability to apply science and logic.

43. Consciousness and sense of mind.

44. The ability to discern or the subconscious.

45. Aesthetics, which includes the ability to see beauty and creativity music, design, literature, and drama.

46. It is a psychic ability that includes the ability to foresee, clairvoyance, psychokinesis and clairaudience. projection, and perhaps certain animal instincts as well as sensitivities to plants.

47. The sense of astral and biological time and awareness of the past, present and future things.

48. The ability to seduce other animals.

49. Relaxation and sleep , which includes meditation, dreams, and consciousness of brain waves.

50. A sense of pupation, including the creation of cocoons and metamorphosis.

51. A feeling of stress that is excessive and the feeling of capitulation.

52. The sense of survival that comes from joining with a well-established group.

53. Spiritual sense, such as conscience, the capacity for perfect feelings of love, ecstasy, feeling of sin, deep pain and sacrifice

54. The sense of unity, of attraction that is the one primordial essence that is the source of all other senses.

Courtesy: SCRIBD

The work is a demonstration of the levels of significance and complexity that can be found, even when we've barely begun to explore our full potential.

Discussions about multidimensional awareness have been a major topic in psychospiritual circles for a long time, and there are many theories and frameworks attempt to understand things that are in their nature, irrational and nonsensical. In order to construct an attainable modality within the infinite possibilities We have simplified our notion of reality to the simplest interface that can be used to access human consciousness. This is what we refer to as Astral Space.

ASTRAL SPACE vs PHYSICAL SPACE

Astral Space contains all thoughts and feelings, as well as fantasies, dreams, memories visions, thoughts, and other experiences within; that is, everything that is not easily controlled by the laws of physics as we understand them. The term technically refers to "of the stars" however, it's an immediate experience. the moment you close your eyes and begin to imagine or recall that something, we're entering Astral Space. It is sometimes called "four-dimensional awareness" which is our own personal Astral Space. We all have an Astral Body, also known as a light body, that can be used to navigate the Astral Plane by using the creative, imaginative aspect of ourselves (see Volume III of Expansion).

Every object has an astral shape. We are able to "see" astral shapes of three-dimensional objects using our deep holographic memory. It's possible to see that an object's or a person's astral appearance is different from its physical appearance. These variations provide important details about the object's nature and our relationship to it. When we view the third-dimensional space from an astral viewpoint it is possible to understand more deeply what we believe of, feel and believe about the world surrounding us.

What makes physical things more than astral is the ability to predict its behavior. All that we experience using our normal senses is considered to be physically real because we are able to predict its behaviour through the same mathematical principles, for instance, The Laws of Thermodynamics. When a thought transforms into an action or word, it transcends the astral and into physically-based reality. It is this process through which everything is born into physical reality.

Astral phenomena, however aren't so simple to determine, however certain "laws" are applicable. In the absence of understanding these concepts the thoughts, feelings and memories, as well as dreams and extrasensory visions can be inexplicably interspersed and we are left in a state of confusion as we try to comprehend our experiences.

THE POWER OF THE MIND

As sentient beings living in the Akashic Field, we are able to extend our consciousness to experience nearly unlimited levels of perception across the spectrum of our own consciousness and the entirety of consciousness. When we expand our awareness beyond our body and immediate surroundings, we are aware of all the beings which surround us, such as humans, animals and plants, as well as insects and other subtle creatures we encounter. We might care about these creatures or not but they are an integral essential to our existence. They share in the basic joy of living. We are able to continue expanding our awareness to the scale of continent, nation and world, the galaxies, solar systems, the universe and beyond, including alternate dimensions and many more.

The key to gaining access to this expanded awareness is called "imagination" that we prefer to refer to as "astral consciousness". A very potent features of Astral Awareness is its human capacity to imagine any object, space or even being in Astral Space. The concept of "astral engineering" is often known as visualization.

To awaken our Astral Awareness and improve our visualization abilities We don't need to do anything extra to do it. We just let our minds to perform what they are best at and that is to wander. Let that child in us that has been buried by years (or years) of boredom as an adult to play and discover the connections that exist in Astral Space.

Astral awareness isn't a simple process for anyone. It is most of the time it is because of the notion the difficulty of visualization. Fortunately, experiences in the astral realm are not necessarily visual. They typically express themselves as emotions or memories, as music, colors, shapes or even as patterns. But symbolic language, which is dream language represents the closest way to connect with the unconscious mind. Visual representations therefore are extremely important in Astral Space.

It begins with simple visualization, by imagining a single object and letting the subconscious fill the blanks. The form, color or the appearance of the "imaginary" astral ball can vary from one person to the next and have radically different associations and trigger a variety of physical and emotional reactions. We strive to "force" as few specifics as we can, creating an astral structure which is also known as a "bucket" and leaving the subconscious to complete the rest. This is the fundamental Akashic reading process. What's in the bucket , if we don't add something to it?

TRANCEWORK SCRIPT 02: EXPERIENCING AWARENESS

INSTRUCTIONS

Take note of the get your feet on the ground prior to attempting this exercise! It is possible to experience some confusion in case you're not familiar with Trancework.

This exercise can help you create an astral space that is based on your physical environment. Let go of the need to think about everything and let the mind go where it would like to move.

It is possible to go through the possibility of recording a Guided Journey to deepen this experience.

SCRIPT

Find a comfy location in an area you are familiar with.

Your bedroom, your living room...someplace that you are at home, somewhere familiar. You are familiar with all the furniture in this room at a certain level even though you don't even realize it.

Let yourself reach the state of trance at which you are most at ease. Relax, breathe and let yourself relax.

Then, open your eyes and take a look at the surroundings.

Learn the information visually regarding the space. Recall everything you know about objects here. What is it they are there for? Are you a fan of these things? Are there any decorations? Photos or other keepsakes? Stones or crystals? What furniture do you have? Are there plants? Do you have pets around, or perhaps others? Let yourself take into consideration all the visual information surrounding you.

Close your eyes, and imagine what you just witnessed in great detail by imagining it in your mind's eye within your astral awareness.

Rebuild and build this space in your Astral Space.

Spend some time and think about the things you see in your vicinity as well as you can.

Explore the space. Are there objects that appear differently from Astral Space than they do in the physical world? If yes, investigate the implications of this by engaging your senses, and most importantly how you feel.

While your eyes are closed, now you can use all your senses. What are you able to feel, smell, hear and feel? Do these sensations come from the natural world or are they physical? Set these sensations in the boundaries of your Astral Space.

Now focus your attention on your body.

Start with your feet first and look around your body all the way to the top the top of your head. Imagine the various areas of your body in Astral Space. What is your body like as it appears in the Astral World? What are the colors and shapes of the various areas in your body? Do you notice symbols or even textures on certain areas or your entire body? Now, observe what you notice; note without judging.

Then extend your attention towards the structure you're in , and the people around you. No matter if you're familiar with they exist or not you're linked to them through numerous ways. Imagine what they're doing. Imagine what they are thinking or feeling. Are there any shapes or colors surrounding them?

Make yourself more aware towards your entire nation. What are the people who are in these countries? You could share an underlying language or a common culture. You could be related to a lot of them. Let yourself be a part of the benefits of this Cultural Awareness.

Then expand your knowledge to the whole continent. Be aware of the diverse different cultures, people, animals and plants, the geographic features, and other features of this continent you reside on in this vast land mass. Get connected to the world through your Continental Awareness.

In the next step, open your eyes to the whole world. Be aware of Mother Earth, the Earth fully. Everyone you cherish and everything you've accomplished or cherished during this lifetime are here in this universe the blue and green sphere that's moving across space. You can be in the world of Planetary Consciousness, an awareness of everything in the world of Earth. Be aware of the movement and the flowing mineral and the hot core.

Then, extend your consciousness to the whole solar system. Be aware of the warmth of sun, and the distinctive nature of every planet. When you travel through them all, experience their power and ancient splendor - these are the gods of the ancient past. Explore them as as you'd like to while expanding your knowledge towards the entire solar system. You are now part of the solar system, and you gaze out at space.

Connect to the stars. Experience their energy and their distinctive character, and their impact. Take a few minutes to be with your Star Awareness joining with many other star clusters in the space. Feel their vibrating, their music and their frequency.

Now , connect your consciousness to the whole galaxy. It is the Milky Way, floating in the vast universe, with billions of stars. This awareness is an integral part of you as the fact that you are an integral part of the Milky Way. Feel the enormous energy churning out of your core and out into your distant arms, soaring across time. You are experiencing Galactic Awareness.

For a brief second, be the universe! Increase your awareness to everything that is. You will realize that you share the same consciousness with as the universe. You are only a tiny speck There is no separation. This is Universal Awareness.

Then, step back down the spiral of consciousness to the universe now and all the way to solar systems right now and down to earth right now, and into your body and into your bedroom to relax in a state of peace for whatever time you like.

Chapter 3: Safe Trancework Practices

Safety is the main aspect to consider when working with Trancework. It is important to be kind, thoughtful and compassionate, but in the end, non-judgmental when we engage in these deeply introspective practices.

To achieve this we have come up with seven fundamental practices that will make sure that you are safe.

THE SEVEN COMMITMENTS TO TRANCEWORK SAFETY

We will adhere to these seven principles when actively participating actively in Akashic Trancework. There isn't a priority here. All are equally important and interconnected.

* Breathwork

* Grounding

* Emotional Management

* Thought Management

* Self-care

* Physical & Astral Boundaries

* Support System Engagement

EXPLORING THE SEVEN COMMITMENTS

BREATHWORK

Anyone who is experienced with yoga or other exercises which incorporate breathing exercises may know the basics such as diaphragmatic breath and breath as a life power (prana). Alongside the techniques we offer, incorporating daily pranayama techniques such as the Breath of Fire and Alternate Nostril Breathing can keep the body balanced and well-nourished.

The practice of breathing is crucial to managing the stress response while remaining connected to your body in both the Trancework Journey , and in general the daily life. Since breathing is so crucial and since the majority people do not breathe in a proper way and properly, we devote a whole Lesson to investigating breathing as an essential and efficient method of general relaxation as well as a method to quickly induce certain state of trance.

GROUNDING

The practice of grounding is a part of Akashic Trancework, the term "grounding" is the process of remembering that we are living beings experiencing a physical experience. It could be as easy as a walk with your feet on the Earth or taking the time to relax and breathe as you do household chores in a mindful manner or even playing with your child or pet. The act of grounding creates a balance in our physical bodies by which helps coordinate the electrochemical process and creating the feeling of calmness.

When we are working within Astral Space, developing a regular practice of grounding is essential to ensure that our physical bodies are healthy and that our Astral Space maintains energetic integrity. The practice of grounding is the fundamental element of safe Trancework. It's taught more deeply In Lesson 0.

EMOTIONAL MANAGEMENT

From a practical point of view from a practical point of view, emotional management is among the primary goals for Akashic Trancework. People who are intuitive, creative and are attracted to astral awareness as well as being referred to as empaths Highly Sensitive People seers, witches or geniuses and lunatics are often struggling with emotional and psychic boundaries. The emotional and inner environments of these individuals can be chaotic and uncomfortable and sometimes without warning.

Being conscious in Astral Space allows us to gain a greater understanding of our emotions and subconscious obstacles. If we are able to approach this area with awareness we can create individualized specific, practical methods for healing and managing our emotions.

THOUGHT MANAGEMENT

Since intentional thinking is the main tool in Trancework the ability to channel our mental energy in a constructive manner is crucial.

When we concentrate on something we focus on it, we give it our attention and energy. We're committing time to it , and we allow it to be part of our private Astral Space. In the event that our thought patterns are generally positive, there's nothing to worry about; it's the mind's conscious doing what it's required to perform. If we're experiencing disruptive or disturbing thoughts, then we're most likely to experience unpleasant Trancework experience. The techniques for managing thoughts offered in these lessons are meant for ensuring that your initial experience will be "clear" sufficient to allow us to move towards progressively higher levels of understanding.

An explanation is needed on meditation. The definitions and methods for meditation vary greatly, and nearly all are useful when they are practiced in a real way. Trancework isn't a form of meditation in the sense that it is, however, it is a method of engaging in meditative state. Traditional meditation techniques allow for the ability to induct (see Lessons 4 6, 5, and 4) to deeper state of mind (see Lesson 1). Individuals who are able to meditate effectively notice that managing their thoughts becomes more effortless in time as they get more comfortable with their thoughts and emotions.

Certain people, however, have a significant difficulty meditating in part due to the notion that they cannot do it. It's similar to the belief that some people hold that they are not attracted to. If we believe that we can't accomplish something, then surely we are not able to. It is the Akashic Trancework answer to each of these beliefs is simple . . . let's not. There is no need to make ourselves meditate or hypnotize ourselves; there are many different ways to feel altered states.

All this is to encourage the initiate to contemplate if it's beneficial, but to not be so absorbed on"shoulds "shoulds" to the point that we lose focus on the reason we're doing it.

SELF-CARE

When we engage in Akashic Trancework, we use our emotions and minds in ways that we may not have been used to. With training, we are able to spend a significant amount of energy to explore Astral Space. Like all disciplines it's essential to understand the limits of our abilities. It is important to remember that we are human beings, and we must take care of ourselves far more than we would normally.

Self-care strategies differ widely. We suggest plenty of good sleeping, lots of fluids and nourishing, fresh food items. We also suggest supplementing Trancework by doing bodywork and exercise. Yoga asana of any kind or other restorative, gentle physical practices work particularly well when combined with Trancework. Even the simplest practices such as dressing, bathing, and grooming are crucial. Therapies like massage as well as sound healing and Reiki can also be beneficial.

Whatever self-care routines that we pick, we need to be honest with ourselves regarding the commitment. If we've never been athletic throughout your life, then the chances of us committing to an intense yoga or running routine every day is quite low. But, if we commit ourselves to something that we know is easy to do such as walking at a mile or performing some basic poses and then progressing to more demanding tasks. The "baby steps" approach to setting goals is a great method to gradually ease into any new routine and respect the body's inherent resistance to changes.

PHYSICAL & ASTRAL BOUNDARIES

We are sovereign creatures, and every one of us has the ability to define boundaries. We (hopefully) have an concept of what it means to set boundaries physically. We determine who is allowed to be near us, talk with us, and enter into our private areas. We also choose what kind of relationships and interpersonal communications we'll allow. The effectiveness we have in enforcement of these rules could be a different issue, but at the very least we have the right to enforce these relationships.

Astral boundaries On the other hand they can be more difficult. If there's a person that is an idea, an idea thought, memory or thought that is that is circulating through our thoughts that is devouring our attention and energy, then we're giving it our attention. It is a typical experience for those suffering from depression, anxiety, and PTSD. We can completely distance ourselves from all people and objects that could make us feel anxious, or we may choose to hide from the world. However, within our heads the disorder persists, always consuming our minds and hearts which consumes our energy and time. It is possible that we have a well-defined physical boundaries, but have no notion of the astral boundaries.

These kinds of extreme cases typically require some sort of therapeutic help in some form, however the majority of us suffer from these kinds of distortions at times. It's not always negative experiences, but as any parent knows, there are times when we just need to be in a space.

The idea of astral boundaries is more than just security and protection as we investigate our understanding of the Akashic experience. As the foundation of this practice, we've got an entire Lesson that is devoted to investigating the various methods to manage astral boundaries effectively (see Lesson 9). Furthermore, many of the exercises in this Handbook support the idea of creating loving, healthy boundaries to ensure safe Trancework.

SUPPORT SYSTEM

We are not designed to be alone. In deep-level astral practice, the quality of our support system is a major factor on the effectiveness and quality of these techniques. Ideally, we'd be able to connect with our family members for assistance. If possible, we recommend spending time in a conscious effort to be in touch with your spouse, partner and family members, friends and children, or anyone else willing to listen to us as we undergo these transformational experiences. The use of a "sounding board" is a fantastic present, even if our friends don't fully understand what that we're sharing with them.

We know that not all people have "someone" or when we do it is not always an individual we can turn to for help. We might feel lonely or misunderstood. We may even think that we're "crazy" due to how people react when we talk stories of our experiences astral.

Luckily, we have support systems that extend beyond our physical realms. Guides will be discussed to help us in Lesson 8 and in Volume II: Release and also periodically throughout the course. Many ways they are the ones we are able to be able to connect with and understand the in the most authentic way.

Furthermore, a major motive of Akashic Trancework is to create an environment of souls who are similar to each other. We are all from diverse backgrounds but share common stories, skills and desires. We invite all new members to get connected with the community to share a common goal as well as a sense of vision and connection. We cannot emphasize enough how crucial authenticity and openness are essential to the process of learning.

TRANCEWORK SCRIPT 03:

SAFE TRANCEWORK PRACTICE

INSTRUCTIONS

This exercise is a simple astral overview on the Seven Commitments discussed in this Lesson. We suggest revisiting this exercise as you need to. You might want to consider the recorded Guided Journey to deepen this experience.

SCRIPT

Begin to lower yourself to a comfortable state of trance. In any place you feel at ease. Let yourself relax to the point that you're getting comfortable and warm.

Then, you can slip back into the Astral Space. Relax and imagine the energy coming from the bottom of your spine gradually expanding to the floor, roots of light extending deep in the Earth. Be aware of the Earth below you, no matter how distant she may appear to be, she's there.

Feel her Feel the Earth as well as all living things crawling, growing, moving around. You are a part of the Earth. Be aware of how connected you are to everything that is growing and lives. Be aware of your body. Feel your body. What are you hearing this moment?

Then, look for your breath. Allow it to flow naturally into as well as out lung. The air will flow into and out. Try controlling the flow of air into your lungs. After that, let the air to relax by breathing naturally, softly taking note of the breath when it exits the body.

Take a deep breath into your stomach and allow your breath to move. Take note of the sensations that your breath creates. What does your breath tell you about your wellbeing? Pay attention to the message of your breath.

When you are breathing more deeply as you relax take a moment to check in with your feelings. What are you feeling right today? What are your feelings? Take note of what comes up in a non-judgmental way and without tying anything to it or attempting to remove anything. Are you experiencing an emotion you are at ease with? In the event that not, can know what causes you to feel uneasy? Be aware of the emotions that come up. They're messages that comes from the subconscious, your body and soul.

The more you are able to accept the emotions in a positive way and appreciation, the more you'll be able to discern the meaning of emotions to offer. If you attempt to deny and ignore the feelings, then the feelings and images could become more intense and uncomfortable with time.

You are not stifling. You are receiving the blessings of gratitude. If you find the feeling overwhelming, set it aside for a moment. You don't have to put all your effort into trying to comprehend this feeling. You are able to choose the moment to dedicate your time and energy toward a more awareness of yourself.

Check in on your thoughts.

What thoughts are forming in your head right now? Are they phrases and images, or in sound, light color, symbol or light? Are you seeing creatures in your head, individuals you know, or animals? Do you have thoughts that appear to overtake and overpower anything you may be being thinking about?

If so, try to remain present to the thoughts. Don't be judging them, don't remove them But don't bind yourself to them in any way. Take a look at them as cloud formations in the night sky changing shapes and merging, then separating. Naturally, thoughts arise alongside emotions, as well as all the other experiences.

We are taught to direct and control the thoughts of our minds as we get deeper into our Trancework journey.

Make something with your thoughts, something you are passionate about. Utilize your imagination, your imagination, and creativity to create an idea which is more important than what it is that you find yourself battling. Something that is more significant and powerful and more important than whatever you are putting your energy and time thinking about. Let it absorb your energy and eliminate the stress you've been paying attention to other things you've been focusing on for many years. It is a positive thing that will help you feel more confident.

When you are focusing at your thought, try to think of your own body. Imagine it in the same way as you did before. What is the situation? What is your state of emotional well-being? Do you receive the nourishing and replenishing support you are entitled to as an individual being? If you aren't, are you open for the divine in ways you are able to be more open to receiving this? Are you taking good care of yourself? Have you eaten? Do you sleep? Are you drinking enough water? What else should you do to look after your body?

Make sure to check your body for all the different parts of your body.

Are you experiencing some discomfort or pain in any area? This is the perfect time to give that area of your body with unconditional love. The act of sending love can provide immense healing power.

Think about all the areas where you can put your focus. Every single demand that the universe appears to make of you. What percentage of this is your emotional state? How much energy are spending on things that you do not would like?

You have the right to set an absolute limit to anything that consumes your energy, not just your own feelings. You are entitled to an Astral Space in your own that is where you can experience the unconditional love you have for yourself. Locate this space today. Feel the love that is expanding in that heart area. This is the best limit you can set that is the love boundary. If you can face any challenge by lovingly, you'll never be hurt.

Imagine a troublesome individual or situation within your own life. Consider the person or circumstance wholeheartedly, with compassion. If you've suffered harm by someone else, you aren't required to apologize, anytime soon, or except if you choose to. It is important to remember that you do not have to think about it. You are entitled to not to consider things. Even if they're around you at all times and you are surrounded by them, you have the right to avoid having them within the Astral Space.

Whatever it is whatever it is, take it out right now. Tell them to go. Even if you are in love with the person you are with and want to keep them around, you are entitled to now ask them to go away for a while. Be aware that by setting an enduring relationship with the person you love you are teaching that they are their most authentic self.

Think of all those individuals in your lives that provide support to you, who cherish you and nourish you. Be in touch with their feelings of love and experience it in a deep way. If you don't have anyone in your life whom you'd like to reach out to, then connect with your fellow Tranceworkers. We're all connected, we all have a responsibility to help each other. Bring your full energy. If you have already worked with guides or ancestors, or other type of astral being, ask them to join you. If not, don't worry and you'll get to get to know them eventually.

Take a moment to just relax in your Astral Space, connecting with all the love that exists in the universe in any state of trance you are at ease.

Chapter 4: Breathwork

The yogic sciences show us that breathing is a conduit for prana, the primary life force in the universe. When we breathe, we circulate prana throughout our astral and physical bodies activating all of our cells and linking us as one entity that is swimming in the energetic medium which sustains all living things.

Breathwork is a fundamental part of many physical and spiritual practices, just as it is essential to all spiritual and physical practices. The methods we employ for Akashic Trancework are identical to Buddhist Vipassana Meditation practice. We simply observe the breath and notice the way it affects our lives. We build a bond to the breath, since it is our lifeline, at any time.

When we breathe correctly and allow our lungs to expand to their capacity every time we breathe and then releasing fully after every inhalation, our body as well as minds naturally relax. In this state of deep relaxation we begin to concentrate our awareness of the astral. In this way, breathing becomes the primary tool for trance induction that Tranceworkers have to learn to master. Through controlling our breathing we can achieve the state of mind that we desire.

The process involves two steps: we learn to master our breath and also learn to be aware of breath patterns in the Trancework participants and those who need our assistance. Through these sessions, we've noticed an essential connection between the kinds of Trance states that are experienced and the pace of breath. We discovered that, in essence the deeper the trance was, the more sluggish and long the breaths of the person experiencing it were. There are numerous non-verbal signals that provide information about the condition of a person's mind, but breathing is the best visible and reliable gauge of brainwave activity. There will be instances where a person is non-verbal. As a Tranceworker who is effective, it is important to be able to discern these signs easily.

We've created two distinct methods to induce an approximate trance state quickly and efficiently. These techniques are known as Alpha Breath and Theta Breath. The fundamental idea behind this process is a kind of biofeedback, which utilizes specific breath counts in order to create the brainwaves associated with it. It is a way of re-creating the breathing patterns that take place in our natural state of mind. the various states.

Check out each method below. The actual number of breaths counted could differ based on the capacity of your lungs and your ease of use. It can be beneficial to ask someone else for a count first. It is helpful to count in the breath "count into" of breath is a powerful technique for trance-induction when working with strangers.

ALPHA BREATH

Inhale for 5 seconds then pause for 2 seconds and exhale for 5 count.

The number of participants could be different between 4-7.

In Lessons 1 and 2, Alpha Trance is when we first begin to tap into Our Astral Space to use our creativeand imaginative skills constructively. The majority of the activities in the book can be done in this state.

THETA BREATH

Inhale for 7 times Then pause for 3 seconds and exhale for 7 count.

The count can vary from 6-9.

As we've discussed in Lessons 1 and 2, Theta Trance is often referred to as the "sweet area" in Trancework. Theta is the place where we usually go through the deep journeys that associated with Trancework and also the state that we experience when we're in a dream state.

STAYING AWAKE

Although Alpha Breath is easy and normal for most individuals, Theta Breath can be an unintentional trap. When we are relaxed this deeply, we naturally desire to descend to a deeper delta state. This is not a problem. this, and often an euphoric state is what we require. It is possible to slip into delta states whenever we need complete rest and replenishment from trauma, stress or everyday stressors. Delta states are a wonderful location to receive healings that need minimal involvement for the practitioner, like the use of sound healing or Reiki however it isn't particularly suitable for Trancework since these states tend to be non-communicativeand can be able to erase the memory of any state of theta that we've had.

The ability to stay awake while self-inducing a theta-like state is vital if we wish to experience multidimensional experiences and return something. Breathing is a extremely simple method to achieve this. We suggest you explore the various breathing patterns and observe the they affect your awareness. Seek out the state of relaxation before falling asleep. It is possible to think of this as "dancing at the edge of a dream" to express poetry. We would like to enter the deepest state of consciousness that we can possibly experience and then return with something special.

TRANCEWORK SCRIPT 04: EXPLORING THE BREATH

INSTRUCTIONS

In this exercise, you'll be observing your breath and all it has to offer you. It is possible to observe your breath at any moment but this is a chance to spend quality time with this part of yourself. You must be in a peaceful, calm location, although you may appreciate doing this exercise when you are sitting, moving or even performing other tasks like cleaning or working. Spend your time in your breath as you can. It is possible to go through the recording of a Guided Journey to deepen this feeling.

SCRIPT

Find a comfy place where you are able to breathe comfortably and unwind without interruption. You can either sit or lay down however you like. Your eyes may be shut or open.

Begin by watching your breathing. Find the place that it enters your body. Select a focus point that you can be able to feel the breath. It could be within your nose, your chest, or in your diaphragm. It could be located inside your stomach. It isn't important. Find a spot in which you be able to feel your breath and your body.

Take some time to think about your breath. Try to figure out how you can regulate your breathing. You can restrict it. You can push it. You can breathe deeply into your chest, or into your stomach or both. You can also hold it for a while. You can alter the speed at which the exhalation and inhalation occur. You can play with your breath a little. Do not do anything that is uncomfortable or hurtful. Just think about what you could deliberately do through your breath.

Release the pressure to manage your breath. Allow it to flow effortlessly. The air will move freely through your lungs while you exhale and inhale. Simply let the air perform its job and fill you up with energy. Move through your abdomen bit, the energy when you breathe naturally. It is being fed into your body by the universe. Inhale the energy you need in the moment, and allow any you don't require to be released with the next breath.

Continue to watch. What does the flow of breath feel within your body? What do the natural flow of your breath affect your body and your mind? What is the consistency or frequency of your breathing patterns? What does your breath tell you about your overall health? Take note of your breathing as it moves through your. It will be sending a message to you to improve your wellbeing.

Take as long in observe and be present with your breath.

Begin to imagine the breath as it moves through your body. Does your breathing appear at the astral level? Does it have a shape or color? What color does it take on when it is absorbed into your body? What do you think it will appear to be like after it goes out? Try moving it throughout your body. Breathe deeply into any area which is experiencing pain or discomfort. Bring the desire for healing to the location along by breathing.

Select a specific pattern to concentrate on within your breathing. All you need be doing is to count your breaths , and stop for a second in after each one. You can select any cycle you like. A four or three, or ten. Be consistent. Make sure to count every breath. Every breath you exhale and inhale is a breath.

Keep a note in your head of the way it feels while breathing in a particular pattern. If the pattern is uncomfortable, you can try something different or simply stop breathing and relax naturally.

Take a moment to spend some time watching and playing with your breath. You can allow yourself to fall into a the deep delta state, or decide to return to a relaxed alpha state, allowing you to start your day with energy, optimism and energy.

Chapter 5: Vocal Toning

Sound, or more precisely, vibrating, constitutes the main organizing basis of physical structure.

As we can observe in the field of cymatics science, sound arranges matter by its frequency and the pattern that it is vibrating. The more precise the frequency pattern more intricate the structures that are created. In Figure 5.1 illustrates this idea using the classic salt table experiment, first carried out by Robert Hooke in 1680. The salt is poured out in random patterns on plates made of metal. A bow is played on the plates producing a spectrum of frequencies that vibrate salt in various designs across the table. The lower frequencies are first played and create a basic fundamental geometric symmetry. Note how complex the pattern grows when higher frequencies are played.

FIGURE 5.1 - HOOKE SALT TABLE EXPERIMENT.

Consciousness is an complex structure that is vibrating in an interval from .5 (2) Hz (Deep Theta) to 42 Hz (High Gamma). The electromagnetic waves are necessarily distinct from sound waves and many people make use of music to induce various state of mind. This can range from the application of specific instruments like Crystal Singing Bowls, to electronic biofeedback tones that are produced as binaural beats or isochronic beats and even more. We recommend looking into these tools for their profound healing effects.

Instructional Journeys are layered with theta binaural sounds to aid the Initiates in Trancework Entrainment. We also frequently employ Crystal Singing Bowls when working directly with clients and students, as well as to aid in personal growth and healing. However, as efficient as these instruments are, they are not a substitute for the healing power of human voices.

TONING FOR TRANCE

Vocal toning is the process of using your voice to create certain trance states through vibration through specific points of the body. This simple and effective induction method can be used anyplace, without the need for any special equipment or other demands. Like breathing it is possible to access any state of consciousness through discovering the places in our bodies to tune. It is as basic as humming with a child to sleep and is easy for the majority of people. Although it might be a bit musical but toning isn't singing. It doesn't need to be musical, or even audible and it isn't a matter of how "good" it sounds. Toning is all about sensing the vibration of your voice inside the body.

You can also use words when we are singing or toning our voice, or simply produce the sound as the sound of a hum, or any other word that we like. The goal is to alter the frequency (how it is high, or how low can be) so that you can feel the tone in different locations in the body. For instance, we could produce a middle range pitch and, more likely, will feel the vibrations within our chest. If we hit a high pitched tone, we'll feel it in our head.

Utilizing mantras, words or chants or any other sacred words or phrases adds a new dimension to our toning practices. When we chant a particular mantra or name to adjust our awareness in tune with the frequency that is associated with the mantra or the words we chant. It is often said that "the power of gods is the sound it makes in the name". When we say a names with confidence, conviction and faith and give it the physicality.

We do not give specific chants or mantras for initiates. We believe that every being has to determine their powerful sacred words and names by themselves or using an aid. We encourage experimentation with various tonalities, mantras and names, to see how each one is unique to the consciousness

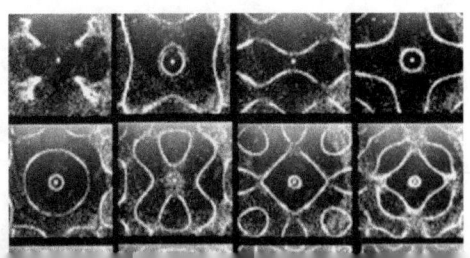

experience.

Similar to breathing exercises, we've seen specific patterns during toning exercises that appear to trigger various states of consciousness. The actual sound matters less than the pitch, and also where within the body the frequency is felt. It is a technique that can be intuitive which is why we encourage experimentation using different volumes, pitches and durations. The mouth can be open or closed and the sound shouldn't be forced. Instead, it is best to "ride the breath out softly" and give a pleasing and tingling sensation within the body, where the sound is focused.

How long you need to tone for is an individual matter. Each tone must occur as a result of a full breathing cycle. This can vary based on lung capacity.

ALPHA TONING

AREA: The head, with the centered on the nasal cavity.

To trigger Alpha Trance, we begin to tone our head using a high-pitched sound. You will feel a tingle within our jaw, face and even in our skull. The majority of alpha states stem from toning to the highest frequency we can easily sustaining. If performed correctly this method should result in an euphoric, yet conscious state.

THETA TONING

AREA Torso located between the solar plexus and the coronary artery.

To experience the Trance state We tone your middle and feel the energy between the solar plexus and our heart. You will feel yourself calmer than with higher pitch tones, and you may begin to get images or thoughts from the subconscious. This is a great way to induce states of theta quickly, without the use of external sources.

TONING BEST PRACTICES

* Don't force the tones. You should work within your natural range.

* Breathe! Keep diaphragmatic breathing in mind - deep belly breaths.

Toning should be done when lying flat or sitting upright with a good air flow.

Don't be concerned about sounding professional. You're not performing. You are simply experiencing your own personal music. Relax and enjoy it. Let it get a little weird. Inform your family members or friends!

Do not stop immediately when you feel short of breath or uneasy. Toning should be a relaxingand enjoyable experience.

TRANCEWORK SCRIPT 05:VOCAL TONING

INSTRUCTIONS

Today's workout focuses on exploring your vocal tract. It is expected that you be active! Sound! Try to be as relaxed as you can. Vocal toning is an inducement which means that you are changing your awareness when you practice this. It is recommended to start with a light Alpha Trance and experimenting with the various ways to alter your perception using your voice.

You might want to look into the possibility of recording a Guided Journey to deepen this experience.

SCRIPT

Find a comfortable and relaxed spot in a location that offers lots of privacy and peace. Simply take a few pleasant simple breaths to get yourself into an alpha-like Trance.

When you feel relaxed and relaxed, start to hum. You can hum along or simply create an sound. Be aware of the vibrations that accompany the sound. Notice how your lips feel. Take note of the way your stomach is feeling. Take note of the way the chest is feeling. Take note of the amount you breathe, and how it affects your experience of the sound you are making.

Breathe deeply and then explore the humming process slightly more. You can alter the sound depending on the location you concentrate on your breath. What is the sensation within your head? What about your throat?

Make time to look at sounds that you can create.

When you hum and ton, let yourself be able to hear your own voice. What other sounds surround you? What are they and how do they alter in response to the sounds that you are creating? Incorporate those soundscapes into the Astral Space. Listen to them, tone-wise. What are the sounds that affect your feelings? What do the sounds you're making make you feel? What do they mean to you? impression?

Then, look at the tones in the space of Astral Space. What do the sounds you create appear like? What color do they come in? What shape do they have? How do they affect you Astral Space? What happens to you Astral

Space as you make these sounds? Are you altering the shape of your Astral Space with these sounds?

Spend a few minutes to explore the full potential in your vocal tract. Your mouth should be open and you can allow your voice to express fully the sounds that are natural. Do not try to sing or act. Simply express yourself, regardless of the way it sounds. Consider how the various sound effects your consciousness of both the physical and astral.

Spend some time exploring the soundscape. Once you're ready to go to sleep, you can drift into an euphoric relaxation state to sleep until you're ready to wake up.

Chapter 6: Vocal Induction

Note: Before inducing others to do the same:

• Be familiar with safe Trancework Methods (See Lesson 3.) as well as The Akashic Trancework code of ethics.

Be aware of state laws regarding introduction of states that have been altered.

• Always be sure to share your knowledge level to anyone you interact with.

The most important thing is to operate from the deepest part of compassion and discernment whenever someone else is trusting their thoughts to you.

The use of voice to trigger states of trance is part skill part talent and part of intuition. Over time, humans have developed the ability to alter consciousness using basic vocal techniques. Generals, prophets, kings politicians, philosophers businesspeople, and performers were masters of the art of communication before concepts like hypnosis or Neuro-Linguistic Programming (NLP) ever existed. The current forms of these techniques are built on research conducted by Milton Erickson (1901-1980), who was the first to master these skills in a therapeutic setting and is widely considered to be the leading authority on hypnotherapy in the present.

Much of the work that was written around the huge Ericksonian Hypnosis theory was not created by Erickson. Instead, his followers took the ideas and adapted them through observation of his methods. Erickson developed his techniques in a way that was intuitive, and he did this through his interactions with students, patients, as well as (probably) him. It was an Akashic practice. When asked about the method he used to achieve what was he doing, he said, "You just have to listen to your subconscious." Erickson believed that what made his method work was not as important as the effectiveness of them. He relied on other people to understand and explain the mechanisms of his method.

The vast majority of the field of hypnosis is founded on the channeled wisdom of Erickson similar to how the current New Age movement was built on the channeling of spirits like Edgar Cayce and Abraham-Hicks. These are big names with entire systems of belief built around their names. When we look at the work of these giants, we wonder what they do that others do not? Why do they have to spend their whole lives researching their methods?

The answer is easy that they were able to be attentive to their own voices.

Self-trust is the key to managing and working with others in Trancework. We have to be aware of our own thoughts. We are unable to serve others with empathy and non-judgment in the absence of ourselves and speak to our voice. It is essential to pay attention to the way we feel because regardless of whether we're aware or not, the emotions reflect into our voice. If we're unhappy with ourselves, at the very most in the moment how can we try to assist others in achieving that?

YOUR VOICE IS YOUR FRIEND

The Akashic Trancework is not an hypnosis or NLP technique in and of itself however we do incorporate several of these elements into our method of practice. Instead of instructing methods to "fool" your mind to enter a state of trance which is usually used in modern methods of hypnosis and NLP courses, Trancework engages full trance induction. We're making use of our consciousness of voice in order to take ourselves into a state of mind where we can help others. When we're able to let go of this, our communication occurs naturally. Tone speed, pitch, and tone are a thing of the past; we don't need to plan since we've established a relationship with our voice. Once we've established this connection and become familiar with it, we can be attentive to subtle signals and cues in the person who is inquiring, like eyelid movements and breathing.

A majority of people aren't thrilled with how they sound with their personal voice. It's likely that you've experienced the sensation of "nailing" an anthem in the shower and then hearing yourself on a tape and feel like an animal who has been injured! Even if you're a talented singer singing, reading loudly can make us feel uncomfortable. It is recommended to record the scripts from this book and replaying them while observing the voice within the context of the various aspects discussed throughout this Lesson. This will allow you to establish an active listening connection to your voice. If we are able to find the "friendly" tone which makes us feel comfortable when we hear it then we've found the voice that is Trancework!

Try this Do this: Be attentive!

The following sentence is a good example:

"Six ball bouncing in the air breathed gently down seven steps."

The words aren't clear, but that's not a problem. Pay attention to your voice. Are you clearly speaking or stumble over words? Are you slurring or racing? Are you speaking the syllables correctly? What is the location of the inflection in each word?

In order to master Vocal Induction, we begin by paying attention to the way we sound when we talk. Then we realize that the state of our awareness is affected by the way we talk about things more, or more than we actually say. Although volume and timbre are important in vocal induction it is evident that they occur naturally when we concentrate on the tone, pitch, and the speed. In this Lesson we'll examine the specific aspects in Vocal Trance Induction in depth. Check out Volume III for more information about the more intuitive aspects of leading other students.

THE BONES OF VOCAL INDUCTION

As we've mentioned, paying attention to our personal tone, pitch and speed can help us modify our voice in order to create Trance-like states in ourselves and other people. Let's look at what each of these aspects contributes to the process of induction.

TONE

In linguistic communication is the character or quality of what we're speaking. This can be defined as words, inflections accent, and other characteristics that convey emotion, purpose and other non-verbal messages. We all know the distinction between a sarcastic happy sad, happy or vocal tone. Tone is even a factor in writing.

A quality of sound Tone refers to one consistent sound that is a single, consistent. It isn't completely independent of tone in the sense of linguistics since tonal shifts in speech can alter the tone of a verb.

These are the best methods to use tone for vocal inductions:

The focus should be on the idea of communicating warmth. Make sure you use a calm, soothing as well as steady tone of voice.

Avoid a sharp emphasis when you talk. Make sure you smile and look frowny when you speak. Watch how your tone changes.

Be mindful of your words. Be precise, genuine and concise. Beware of the temptation to explain too much, apologize, or revert. If you fall, just persevere. If you stumble or cough Keep going. Rely on your voice.

Make sure to emphasize the things that are significant. The inflection should be placed on the key concepts and words. Make sure to lengthen the last syllable whenever it is appropriate.

* Repetition, rephrase and repeatedly, and repeat any key concepts. Find a rhythm that is natural to repetition. Repeating something at least three times allows an unconscious mind to take in the idea.

Listen as if you're in the room. When you're trying to convince you or someone else to listen to listen, active listening is essential to propelling forward on the Journey forward.

Every moment provides the details that guide you towards the next. This is the most powerful practice of presence (see Volume III Expanding).

* Adjust your tone according to the space. When provoking themselves and other people, Tranceworkers align their energy with the requirements of the journey and the person who is in the trance. Flexibility and emotional flexibility are essential.

* Relax. Do not force phrases to flow. Take a deep breath between each sentence. It's better to speak three powerful, meaningful things than to say a dozen that aren't really relevant or could create confusion. Don't be compelled to say something and let the words flow.

PITCH

Pitch is the way that the frequency of a sound is to the human sense. Pitch refers to the sensation of frequency. As such high-pitched sounds indicate an extremely high frequency sound wave. We perceive a lower frequency sound wave as"lower note. "low tonal". Higher pitched sounds are more likely to cause anxiety and stress and anxiety, while low pitched sounds are relaxing and soothing. The pitch of the voice is altered deliberately using various areas that comprise the vocal tract. Vocal Toning is the process of vibrating the voice through various body parts lets us manipulate pitch to create specific effects (see lesson 5).).

No matter if you have a high-pitched or deep voice you can use you vocal range in order to create altered states of consciousness. Be aware of the following when you think about pitch in vocal induction:

Modify your pitch in accordance with the direction you're heading. For instance, if you're going into a state of Trance, begin with a higher pitched pitch and gradually lower your voice. Begin with a low pitch and gradually increase to signal greater states of mind for instance when you are at the end of your Journey.

The consistency of pitch is crucial. A moderate, pleasant pitch that falls in the middle of our vocal range is perfect for Trancework. You might notice this pitch somewhere in between the heart chakra and the solar plexus chakras. It is usually the best pitch for triggering Theta Trance (See Lesson 5).

Natural pitch is the ideal. Do not force yourself into an articulation that isn't at ease and at ease. Even someone with a high-pitched voice can create an enveloping tone by staying within their own natural range.

PACE

Pacing in Trancework is the term used to describe the process of increasing or decreasing the speed of speech to trigger altered states. Although it may sound simple but conscious usage of vocal pacing is powerful tool to quickly and easily provoking certain states of consciousness. The elongation of words, pauses and deliberate pacing to mimic the breathing and movements of aquerent are just a few methods used by pacing to increase the trance state.

The pacing of vocal Induction can be heard and feels distinct from natural speech. It shouldn't feel boring or dull. It should be stimulating and warm. It isn't easy to get into the slow and more deliberate style of speech required to shift your mind to a different state. It is possible to feel self-conscious or be concerned that we will not "do it correctly". The most important thing to do is to be in tune with the energy in the Journey by focusing on the Journey with all-encompassing presence. When working with a person in person or via video, you should match your pace to the person's breathing, and other non-verbal cues.

Here are some ideas to keep your vocals pacing:

"Slow and steadied" win the race. The slow pace lets us be mindful of our words, as well as pay attention to the tone, pitch and breathing. A slower pace also aids in easing minds into the altered state. When you're on the Trancework journey, it's crucial to allow spaces between sentences and words so that the participant can take in and fully enjoy the experience. Don't hurry even if it seems odd.

Change pacing to change the trance state. The sudden change in pace is the best way to get the person in the state of trance or to draw the person to be more deeply than they are.

The following general rules can be helpful:

* The pacing of Alpha Trance usually feels "normal" and informal.

* The pace in Theta Trance is slower than normal speech, and there is spaces between sentences that allow the listener enough time to take in the information.

TRANCEWORK SCRIPT 06: EXPLORING THE VOICE

INSTRUCTIONS

This practice will allow you to examine tone, pitch and speed in the process of listening to your personal voice. Through practice, you'll be able to alter these elements effortlessly and easily during your vocal inductions as well as in everyday life. If you can, you might consider recording your own exploration of this exercise.

It is possible that you are looking to explore the possibility of recording a Guided Journey to deepen this experience.

SCRIPT

Find a relaxing, comfortable place to sit in. Find an appropriate level of Alpha Trance. This lets you listen and be in touch with in your space.

Breathe deeply and let yourself relax completely. In a minute I'll request you to repeat a few simple sentences.

Be aware of the way you pronounce each word. How fast are you saying them? What tone and tone do you use? What does the language affect you?

Now, repeat after me.

Six balls bounced across seven steps.

I'm relaxed and eloquent.

Nineteen children breathing softly.

Stop the repetition.

Think about how the words sound as you speak each vowel. Did the sentences sound simple and clear? Did you stumble, slur or stumble? It's fine if. Take it slow. Repeat the process after me taking as long as it takes you to finish each sentence, and be certain to pronounce every word.

The giraffes chased eleven baby giraffes and three newborn tigers.

The most crucial aspect of awareness is perception.

Ten highly skilled triceratops attempted to climb twelve trees.

Stop repeating yourself.

Be aware of how these words made you feel as you spoke slowly and with care. What did it feel like in your body? What did it do to your perception of your astral body?

Choose three words with a significant meaning to you.

Speak these words loudly with conviction, intention, and with confidence.

Start now.

Now, stop.

Take note of how these words affect you feel. They affect the way you feel, aren't they? What do they make the mind experience? What do they do to your awareness of your astral body?

Select an expression or sentence that you like or that can make you feel comfortable, at peace and calm or even inspired.

Repeat this sentence again and time and again. Each time you say the sentence, do it in a different way. Try different tones, pitches and pace each time. Examine how the different ways you use the same phrases affect the way you feel.

Take as long as you like performing this exercise. Once you're ready, allow yourself to rise from your trance, being relaxed, calm and relaxed.

Chapter 7: Building your Secure Space

At this point, you should be at ease in triggering state of trance using one or more of the following techniques including breathing as well as vocal toning and vocal induction. The preceding six Lessons offer the fundamental tools needed for us to progress in the A.R.E. Cycle to consider the question how do we enter the trance state, what are we going to do? Now, we're all in a state of solitude with our thoughts emotions, memories, images thoughts, fears and other ephemera from the Astral Plane. What can we do to understand all this?

We go home.

ASTRAL SAFE SPACE

As soon as we put our eyes shut and decide to go into the state of trance, we are confronted with the endless possibilities which lies within. We are able to imagine, recall to calculate, imagine and go through the entire spectrum of human experiences in the tiny fraction of a second in the event that we desire. Utilizing our power to decide the things we focus our attention on, and construct in our astral world and create an uninvolved Space.

Safe Space Safe Space is an "imaginary" space that we imagine within Astral Space. This concept is the base "Purpose Temple" as well as each of our Journey experiences should start and end in this place. We'll talk more on Purpose Temples when we get to Volume II, Release.

A Safe Space can be any lovely, warm, affectionate tranquil place that is easily imagined or recalled. It could be a forest cabin or an island in the tropical zone, or simply the sensation of floating in an unmoving state. It doesn't need to appear "realistic" or even be completely imaginary, such as an animated fairytale. What the space looks like is not as important as the way it feels; it can change from one place to another each time.

The most frequently thought of Safe Space is the beach. The sensation of warm sand between our feet, the glow in the sunlight, the tranquility of the ocean the salty scent that fills our air. All of these memories have positive connotations for the majority of people, and we can use our senses to effortlessly make the experience come to life in our minds' eye.

The most powerful and effective intentional Astral Spaces are built upon positive associations that bring back memories that give us feelings of happiness and joy. To create your Safe Space, we think of the good moments, things we're thankful for and memorable experiences. We allow ourselves to contemplate the ideas, thoughts as well as fantasies, even abstract concepts that give us feelings of security and calm. We let ourselves experience the sensations as we make and feel within the Astral Space. A safe Space can be constructed from everything: objects, shapes colours, scents sound, ideas feelings, thoughts and so on. Think about all five senses when bringing elements to build the Safe Space. The more sensory connections we make with, the more emotions and experiences are available to us as "building substance".

We establish an Safe Space so we have a place to go home regardless of the circumstances we're facing. We don't intend for to use this tool as a means of escape or to bypass spirituality. It is a safe space. Safe Space is our astral "home". Similar to an actual shelter and a sanctuary that we go to to relax, rest and security We also require an Astral Space for this reason. Sometimes, it is referred to as the Astral Temple and our Safe Space should be regarded and considered sacred. In the end, what's more sacred than nourishment for our bodies? Every beginning and end of a Trancework journey with a Safe Space provides a foundation of trust, security and focus. It also ensures that the participant approaches each experiences from a state that is Heart Centered Awareness. We'll go over the importance of travelling from this place in Volume III Expanding.

BIOCHEMICAL REALITIES

Although it's a process of creating the Safe Space astrally, it is a very real. The act of creating the space, nurturing it, and being in this space can have a profound effect on the physical sensations we experience. When we think of positive, nurturing thoughts and feelings, we trigger a biochemical reaction within our bodies. Through activating positive associations and memories, the body releases relaxant chemicals like serotonin, dopamine and Oxytocin. These changes in our body's chemistry alter how we experience, express our thoughts, interact and react to almost everything, coming from a position in Heart Centered Awareness instead of fear.

We often make use of "Safe Space" and "Heart Centered Awareness" in conjunction. This isn't an error or an accident. When we create the Safe Space that we create, we are aligned the body with Heart Centered Awareness. We feel the emotions and body chemistry that express compassion as well as generosity and abundance. In the end, this activates our Gamma awareness, that elusive state of happiness that needs to be developed rather than accessing at will as in Alpha as well as Theta Trance. We'll go into more detail on the significance of Heart-Centered Trancework and awareness when we get into the expansion phase.

TYPES OF SAFE SPACES

Safe Space Safe Space is one of the most customized experiences available to those who are Journeyers. Keep in mind that this is our home astral. It is a tremendous satisfaction to create this space. And the process could take years as it changes and expands. This is a constant flow of inspiration and happiness!

To encourage exploration, we offer the following list of the most common safe Spaces.

Beach. It is perhaps the most well-known Safe Space for beginning Journeyers Experiences at the beach often have the warmth of a warm, relaxing, and pleasant feelings. The water can be an unforgettable experience!

Cabin. A tranquil log cabin or perhaps situated on the summit of a mountain can be relaxing and easy for many of us to imagine.

Cave. Natural, beautiful caves frequently show up on Safe Space Journeys. Certain people appear to have a special place for these caves.

House. A cozy, comfortable house can be a calming experience, particularly for those who do not have the ideal living conditions in their the physical space.

Castle. The art of capturing an elaborate palace or temple can be enjoyable and inspiring and can be an excellent practice in visualization.

Floating. Physical representations don't need to be present when they aren't helpful. Sometimes, allowing ourselves to experience an ethereal sensation like floating we were floating in space or in water could give us the tranquility we require.

Light. Being able to experience and/or observe the light in various patterns and colors, could be deeply relaxing for many.

Sound. We suggest you create soundscapes within your home or discover ways to integrate music and sound in Your Safe Space, especially if you're a musician.

TRANCEWORK SCRIPT 07:

BUILDING YOUR ASTRAL SAFE SPACE

INSTRUCTIONS

We suggest creating Theta Trance to perform this visual workout. It might be beneficial to write down or talk what you experienced afterwards. It is also possible to look into recording a Guided Journey to help integrate this activity.

SCRIPT

Find a comfortable spot to relax to the level that you feel most comfortable and relaxed and allow you to visualize things in your head.

Relax and take a few deep breaths and let yourself unwind a little.

Once you're done, you can imagine your ideal safe and happy spot. It could be any location either real or imaginary as abstract or physical as you want. It could be a place you've been to before or one you'd prefer to be or a location you design entirely from your imagination.

Imagine yourself in this secure, peaceful space. Here , there aren't any distractions, no obligations and no pressure. It is a space to unwind and reconnect with your own self. This is the space of greater self-awareness and Heart Centered Awareness.

Relax and take a few deep breaths and relax even more deeply into this space. Spend some time absorbing all the senses you can experience here. What are you hearing? What are the sensations you feel on your skin? What smells do you detect? What are you doing here? Explore this area by using your senses.

Spend some time today to make this place. Include the right objects that are shapes, colors, ideas, thoughts, light. Anything can make you feel peaceful and peaceful, and full of happiness and love.

If something or someone enters this space and creates a sense of discomfort you can let it go in the present. There will come a time and place for these things that are appropriate. In the meantime, you can just sink in this place of happiness, peace, unconditional love and compassion.

Continue to build the space. If there are any animals or humans who are in the area, that's okay. You can allow them to stay if you would like or request for them to go away. This is your space and you are free to be here , if you wish. The presence of any energy or person is permitted here without your consent. Accept this fact right now.

Take note of how you feel within the space. Keep this feeling in mind. Anytime you can reach this location from any level of consciousness simply by recollecting the way you feel here, and also what it looks like in this place.

Do not worry if you're having difficulty visualizing the Safe Space. It doesn't have to appear like anything that exists in space. It could look nothing whatsoever. It could be just the color of light sound, or any of these things. It could be that you want to feel at peace in your heart without the need to do any sort of creation. That's fine. As long as you are at ease, calm you can return whenever you want to.

Take as long as you want here, unwinding. If you're ready to get up, you'll be able to do it, knowing clearly the way to return here whenever you want to.

Chapter 8: Inviting in Your Guides

Being in contact with guides is among the most powerful, enriching and intimate elements of the spiritual experience. Each of us has unique relationships and perspectives of guides. To aid in our work we define a "guide" as anything that assists us in the boundaries of our Astral Space. Guides could comprise an animal a person that we are fond of or admire, a hero pets, a beloved one who passed away or died, a fictional character or a historical character. Many people have guides that appear to be entities of light or extraterrestrials ancient ancestors, or as mysterious symbols and forms. The color of a concept, or an idea song or even a number may serve as a guide. Our emotions and feelings of anger and anger, as well as things that we consider to be limitations or limitations could act as guidelines.

Guides are an essential element of the work that we've divided our lesson into two sections. In this Lesson we'll be focusing on getting in touch the guides we have. This means meeting new guides and developing connections. In the next volume, Volume II, Release we'll discuss using guides with specific goals.

We realize that not all initiates resonate with the concept of guides. As always, we urge you to be discerning and to respect the limits that let you feel secure and safe. If, however, you decide to do your work without any additional guides or guidance, then we suggest creating a connection with your Lower and Higher Self as a way to practice self-care. The process will be discussed in Volume II of Release.

THE MEETING

When we meet guides, we usually meet guides in the Safe Space (see Lesson 7) However, this may not be the scenario. There are times when we wish to reserve that space for us, or discover that guides appear while we travel across other areas of the astral world. This is okay as long as we are aware that, as with any other being, energy or thought that appropriate boundaries are essential. We'll get into Astral Boundaries in Lesson 9.

It is much easier to connect with guides than most people think. The majority of us are in contact by beings of support who communicate with us every second. Our guides aren't so much about discovering them or bringing them to us. It's more about tuning in to their frequencies and understanding how to recognize and connect with them. We can build intentional Astral Spaces for making connections, which allows us to learn language and build connections between us and our guide.

ARE THEY "REAL"?

It is easy to get overwhelmed by trying to solve this problem, by analyzing and thinking from every angle. Guides can be viewed as real living beings that exist externally from us. Or, discuss them as chemical impulses that are interpreted by our brains as memories recall. Perhaps they're just symbols that our subconscious mind employs to communicate, elements of what Carl Jung called "archetypes" as well as mythical patterns that have a unique significance that we carry in our unconscious.

We don't claim to know the answer. We just don't know. We believe the impact they have upon our life is real and they are likely to be present regardless of whether we'd like they will or not. We recommend listening to messages from guides with a keen eye instead of being concerned on their "realness" that they exist. The value of this experience will be evident.

For some it's not unusual for experiences from guides to "bleed" onto physical space. The mind can be adept at projecting astral events into the physical world. If Michael Talbot has it right the world we experience is an holographic projection of the sensory information that the subconscious mind wishes to perceive.

In the event of this happening this happens, it could be terrifying for the novice

Tranceworker. A careful cultivation of the astral boundaries is crucial (see Lesson 9). There are those who believe that the main difference between the schizophrenics and the shaman is their ability to remove the things that cause us to feel uncomfortable. Whatever is interpreted as a way to guide you whether it is physically or through astrology, should be of clear benefit and should not seem threatening or potentially dangerous. Trust your gut.

COMMON GUIDE EXPERIENCES

Although any thought, emotion sensation, feeling, idea such as these can serve as a guide and influence our lives in significant way, but the best and most effective guides have distinct personas. In the end powerful beings like Thoth, Yahweh, Jesus, Ishtar, the Buddha as well as Archangel Michael. Archangel Michael have led the human archetypal experience over the course of millennia. If these beings are present externally from the inner self, is left for the individual to determine.

The following table lists the most the types of guides that are common. You could meet any of these kinds in physical or astral space. Be aware when you meet new people and establish boundaries and relationships.

ANIMALS

As evident in the earliest rituals of shamanism animals have been leading humans from the beginning of our existence on Earth. Growing side-by-side, the symbolism connection between animals and humans is deeply embedded into our collective consciousness. Sometimes, we get information from animals within Astral Space, or we receive information that is symbolic and inspires us to establish a connection with an animal in order to integrate their energy to our lives. This is commonly called Spirit Animal Medicine.

ANCESTORS

Ancestral connections, whether distant and recent are extremely prevalent, significant guides in many different cultures around the world. In these places, not paying attention to or ignoring the ancestral past is considered to be extremely negative luck. Experiences of astral contact with the ancestral beings are likely to be intense and emotional. The ancestral beings often help us heal old wounds and, at times, seem to require our assistance to "move forward".

ANGELS

Many people connect with angelic figures no matter if they are conventional Judeo-Christian beings or more obscure ones like the angels mentioned by The Enochian Mysteries. Angels are often linked to an appearance of orbs appearing in the physical world.

ASCENDED MASTERS

The Ascended Masters are the educated teachers and sages from the past. A lot of people feel strong connection with these gods like Siddhartha Gautama (the Buddha), Jesus of Nazareth Mary Magdalene as well as Thoth from Atlantis. Sometimes , they are referred as "bodhisattvas" They have achieved enlightenment, however they decide to remain in Earth to assist in liberating all living beings of suffering.

CELEBRITIES & FICTIONAL CHARACTERS

We all were raised watching television. As kids, we were taught about the world via stories from films, books and television, forming our identity in the personas and personalities we watched on a regular basis. No matter what they are, these characters can have a profound archetypal meaning for aiding us in understanding and understand our own inner processes. Are there any mythological figures so well-known and recognizable as Superman and as impressive like Luke Skywalker, or as relevant as Katniss from Hunger Games? Did anyone else in the history of mankind create experiences as powerful and inspirational such as Stephen

King, George R.R. Martin, or Steven Spielberg? If such beings or their creations exist within Astral Space in any form and offer assistance as guides, they can be helpful. As always, use discernment.

COLORS, SHAPES, SOUNDS, AND NUMBERS

Abstract elements and symbols may provide deep sources of information and advice. Colors, numbers, sounds and even sounds can be guides and languages by themselves. When you are able to master them, they can be utilized to develop languages that better communicate with other guides or connect directly to your subconscious. Take a moment to be aware of these elements throughout your day and observe the emotions and thoughts that come up as a result. The sensory and physical sensations can provide you with direction.

DEITIES

The most effective and ubiquitous guides are the gods and goddesses. They are direct and powerful channels to the collective consciousness of the archetypal. The collective belief in gods gives them supernatural power over Earthly things. The Theosophists described these beings as egregores. They are thought-forms brought to life through beliefs that are shared. We advise caution and discernment while working with the gods when they are summoned. Once invoked they are difficult to remove.

"IMAGINARY" FRIENDS

A lot of us were surrounded by imaginary friends when we were young children, with distinct personalities and distinct personalities. As we grow older we're taught to ignore these entities as unimportant phantasms of our mind. We who are Tranceworkers understand the extent to which this isn't the truth , and we advocate the reconnection of astral childhood buddies. It is likely that these "friends" are categorized within one of other groups listed in this article.

LIGHT BEINGS & EXTRATERRESTRIALS

Astral awareness usually involves meeting alien beings. It is possible to encounter beings of blue, white or gold light that appear to resonate with different "star frequency". It is also possible to encounter more typical "aliens" with different sizes, shapes and orientations. These guides are , perhaps, the most frequent to appear in the physical world as many people have experienced in person. It doesn't matter if these are real-life accounts, the alien encounters are so frequent as well as visceral and powerful and powerful that we dedicate the lesson on Volume III, Expansion for dealing with E.T.s.

PETS

What creature is more loving and unconditional than a dog? It's not uncommon to meet the old and new pets within Astral Space, often unexpectedly. Pets differ from other animal guides since they're distinct characteristics of a specific being whom we've been bonded; i.e., "Fido" instead of "dog".

Our guides for pets can be fantastic facilitators of Release and also the source of peace during the most intense astral experiences.

TEACHERS & CULTURE HEROS

Teachers as well as healers as well as politicians, healers musicians writers and writers, thought leaders and philosophers are all evident sources of guidance. In the end, whether dead or alive they are a source of inspiration for us and lead by example, often thousands or hundreds of years later after their death. Think about the influence of the ancients such as Lao Tzu, Plato, Socrates, Homer, Leonardo da Vinci or John Dee? We can all get inspiration from the writings by the likes of Dr. Martin Luther King, Maya Angelou, Mahatma Gandhi, Nikola Tesla, or Janis Joplin? We should not overlook the saints who are patron saints who are part of the Akashic Trancework which include Edgar Cayce, Carl Jung, Milton Erickson, and Esther (Abraham) Hicks. They are living in Astral

Space, their influence expanding across the physical bodies. If we can connect directly with them in Astral Space or simply find an inspiration in their lives they serve as invaluable guides.

THE DEAD

Communication with the deceased is sometimes referred to as "mediumship" or a word that has a variety of levels of significance for the majority of people that range from amusement to fear. In many societies the distinction between the ancestors and the spirits of the deceased is not existent. After all, every person who is alive is someone's ancestral ancestor, even if it's not genetically.

Chapter 9: Creating Astral Boundaries

Astral boundaries help us at multiple levels. The process of the division of Astral Space gives us a way of organizing and processing experiences that are usually complicated, confusing and, in some cases, even hazardous.

Think for a second about the world of the physical without limits. It may sound idealistic and even Utopian initially however, the concept doesn't stand up to examination because humans need protection from predators, the elements and (unfortunately) our fellow humans. Shelter is our primary physically boundary. It is a space that allows us to rest and recharge in tranquility and safety. Anyone who's ever been without a house knows precisely how crucial it is for our health to have these fundamental structures built.

The boundaries between people can make the different between harmony or chaos within our relationships and our lives. It is possible to ask people to be quiet, to not speak to us in according to a particular way or limit the the time that we have with them. However, if we're thinking of the person (or thought, memory, idea, or idea) it's because they're within the realm of our Astral Space. If we focus on them by paying attention, we're bringing their energy, and feeding our connection.

Astral boundaries like boundaries that are astral like the Safe Space serve the same role as shelters do physically. They provide us with a place to recharge and relax as well as a refuge from the stress of continuous emotional and mental chatter. These are spaces where we are able to be who we are and fully, free of judgment or pressure. The great aspect of astral boundaries is that nobody or anything can ever erase them without our consent. Contrary to physical boundaries, they can be shattered or broken by forces and beings that are not our own like the many human beings have experienced throughout history.

For the Tranceworker, it's just not enough to just create boundaries between the physical and the interpersonal. It is also necessary to establish practices to protect us while we travel through Astral Space, and to ensure that we are able to be successful, while adjusting to the external environment without difficulty and building the ability to resist those that attempt to drain our energy away. We set boundaries in Astral Space to this end.

RETREAT, NOT ESCAPE

Astral boundaries can be used to regulate the energy we provide to astral or physical beings and our own feelings thoughts, feelings and ideas, as well as intrusive thoughts that consume the mental resources of our. We should not be averse to the ignoring, suppression or the compartmentalization of the energies of these beings, since it is not always effective as anything that is suppressed will eventually be resurfaced and often with a furious violent vengeance. But, we are able to select the amount of time and energy to give to certain issues in order to be able to manage them in a way that isn't threatening our own identity.

Sometimes, we may have to establish boundaries for emotions that are positive and compassionate, but can hinder us from doing the things we must or would like to accomplish. Infatuations that are intense like this one, for instance, could quickly become obsession and overwhelm all other issues if we do not create boundaries on how much attention to devote to even the most tempting love interest.

Knowing the distinction between the astral boundary and compartmentalizing is essential. Astral boundaries can be extremely efficient in dealing with disturbing thoughts, such as those triggered by PTSD, anxiety depression, grief as well as obsessive-compulsive thoughts and other "uncontrollable" thoughts and feelings. But they shouldn't be used to deflect attention from the responsibilities we have, relieve the responsibility of your actions or separate from our emotions. That is compartmentalization, which can have drastic results, leading to psychosis, depression, and gradual dis-integration as the "stuff" in those compartments begins to seep through the inevitable cracks. We're not making compartments instead, we're creating partitions like rooms or houses that have plenty of doors, windows and vents that allow air (thoughts and emotions) to flow through when necessary.

INTERPERSONAL BOUNDARIES

We all have the right to establish any kind of boundary for any person at any time and we aren't obliged to provide reasons for this. Sometimes, we simply need some time to relax, think and reenergize. Highly compassionate individuals particularly benefit from taking a look and creating boundaries with loved family members. An open, compassionate negotiations of boundaries encourages everyone to bring their very best at the table giving the opportunity to connect to others in more genuine, caring ways.

However, some creatures may choose to disregard our boundaries, just as we might choose to disregard theirs. This is something that many of us are in the habit of doing than we would like to admit. Sometimes, we have to accept someone else's love because they've failed to honor our boundaries. This is also an act of kindness because it encourages the other person to "step up" in order to have a place in our lives. The truth is that allowing an individual to harm you is to permit that person to hurt themselves. The statement about the boundary setting procedure is straightforward in this situation:

"I I love you unconditionally, without any conditions, however, I will not let you to hurt you or me."

SAFE ASTRAL EXPLORATION

In Astral Space we may encounter endless combinations of emotions, thoughts ideas, beliefs and energies as well as memories, beings and many other aspects of our mind. Everything that is in our senses is fighting for the most important factor in all of existence which is our attention. What we pay attention to is where our focus is, where our time is spent and where our energy is absorbed and, ultimately, the direction of our lives.

The basic procedure of setting boundaries for astral energy is to decide the direction of this energy in a conscious manner by deciding how long to devote on an astral experience. If we're focusing on the practical aspects of our obligations, thoughts of someone else, or even astral beings that appear to us during our journey, the primary method will be the same: managing time. What amount of time do you give them every day, every week, every month?

Sometimes, these tasks require our attention even if we don't like them. Work is one of the most common examples. Most people in our contemporary globe "like" their jobs, but we regularly take work to think and thinking about matters which have nothing to do with our personal lives. We must clearly dedicate some of our time to our jobs, however, it is usually just paid for a limited period of time. What is the point of spending your few spare moments in the day worrying about work? Setting an astral boundary that says "leave work at work" is essential to many in order to ensure we can have time for our families, our friends as well as personal interests.

As we have mentioned as previously mentioned, as mentioned, Safe Space is our primary boundary in Astral Space, however it is possible that we need to establish specific boundaries in certain situations while we explore and experience Astral Space. In this Lesson closes, we will examine various methods for creating efficient astral and interpersonal boundaries. Let's first look at the fundamental principles that govern boundaries in the astral realm.

ASTRAL BOUNDARY GENERAL GUIDELINES

Start and finish each journey in the comfort of your Safe Space.

Be aware of your body and keep it in a relaxed state when you walk forward.

If you feel an increase in the level of discomfort or discomfort, you can use breathing and visualization to bring you in to the Safe Space and then back to a state of awakening.

TECHNIQUES FOR BOUNDARY SETTING

Here is a listing of the most common methods to set boundaries in various contexts. These examples can be used as an inspiration for the development of individual methods that are tailored to the Tranceworker's needs and preferences. beliefs.

ASKING

At times, all we have be able to ask for is the being, energy, or being that we love to let go of the space either temporarily or permanently. We leave them with compassion and love and with the knowledge that we are able to invite them back at any time if we wish.

GUIDES

Guides can be used to hold certain energies at bay, to assist to process or comprehend the meaning of something, or simply help you figure things out.

SHIELDING

The idea of being in a light-filled environment protecting color (white or gold, purple, etc.) is a common astral protection practice. The light is typically viewed as being contained within a certain shape like an egg or sphere, pyramid or any other structure with significance and is quickly created within Astral Space.

PRAYER AND RITUAL

Prayer and ritual practices that are based on a well-constructed belief system (traditional or not) are effective in keeping negative energies out of the way. The more belief and commitment that we put into the process the more effective this "banishing".

TIME IN

Sometimes, the intrusive forces may require some degree of our attention. Like we said, suppression is not the aim of this technique; instead, we should be mindful of allowing the space needed to handle the demands of life and to process our experiences. Instead of battling to shut out the unpleasant (or just boring) astral experiences, we can allocate a certain amount of time per day or week, or even month to focus on. This method of "scheduling time into" allows us to give all of our attention to these energies without guilt, shame or hesitation, as we've set aside a specific period of time to focus on them, and allowing us to make use of the rest of our energy to do other productive and enriching things.

PROCESSING TEMPLE

Like similar to "time to" practice The processing temple is a type of purposeful Temple that we will look at the subject in volume II, Release. The "Temple" can be described as an intentioned Astral Space that is specifically dedicated to dealing with any form of energy that is not easily controlled using the other methods discussed previously, like thoughts and feelings that result due to stressful situations in life or from issues like PTSD or depression, anxiety or compulsive behavior. These emotions should not be ignored; they are signals from the lower Self which must be accepted with gratitude, and then processed in order to recognize the message. This isn't a case of compartmentalization since we aren't denying or ignoring them; we're instead establishing an area of our conscious mind to process and allowing us to look again later to determine whether there is something in the experience that we should be able to comprehend and incorporate.

TRANCEWORK SCRIPT 09: CREATING ASTRAL BOUNDARIES

INSTRUCTIONS

In this session we'll look at some strategies for establishing boundaries between astral bodies. This is best practiced in a relaxed Alpha or deep Trance. Return to this exercise whenever you want to establish boundaries , for whatever reason. You might want take a listen of this recording of this Guided Journey to deepen into the learning experience.

Chapter 10: What Are the Akashic Records?

I

If you're not well-versed in the metaphysical realm it is likely that you don't know what is the Akashic Records are. But, you must as, according to people who agree within the lives of these so-called like figures, every soul has one.

It's first important to understand that The word "Akasha" means to Sanskrit in "surroundings," that's where recorded records are claimed to be. Let's take a stab once more and demolish this bogus notion. It's not supported by medical evidence because the all of our knowledge is in abstract concepts and in invisible planes. In 1875 One of the OG spiritual gangsters known as philosopher and occultist, Helena Blavatsky, founded the Theosophy Society. The group is that she and her pupils should practice Theosophy, an obscure "faith" that she founded together with Henry metal Olcott who was one of the first to switch to

Buddhism. I wrote religion in fees because it's a true philosophical system of beliefs about religion and philosophy as a whole is no longer only a method of evaluating things, but something that you consider as a faith. In tandem, Blavatsky and Olcott tried to present their alternative philosophical philosophies of religion to provide spiritualists a basis to draw upon that was not in line with Biblical convictions, but are nevertheless they were similar.

One of the theories that held sway for a long time after Blavatsky was the idea that there's an invisible force , or astral light, that records every component that we've achieved as well as idea and stated. The concept has since become called the "Akashic information,"" an un-secular library which is based on the most efficient size, but that contains information in is available in all dimensions. If you are able to get involved in philosophical ideas that require you to be in agreement with what you are unable to discern, you're likely competent to explore the concept and gain access to this library. but if you are looking for complex information and rational reasons for this, this concept may sound like something J.Ok. Rowling invented.

"To myself," Giorgi tells Bustle, "[the Akashic Records arethe belief they represent the impressions every count numbers (everything that ever existed or ever existed) are recorded on more subtle levels. This is the implicit recording of the particular. Many refer to it as the'reminiscence from nature.' It's an analogy for organic codings similar to DNA."

Why do we have to be concerned about these issues? Giorgi claims it's an extremely comforting idea when you consider it.

"It's the truth under the surface that provides an explanation for the existence. It's the idea that everything ever existed has an imprint that will remain on the basis of reality. The effects, the imprints can be visible through patterns. As a leaf falls into to a pool of water and causing ripples. Both the water and the leaf have forever changing. The moment of the leaf being thrown into the water is now part of records that are both physical and cosmic." she says . So if you think of yourself as the leaf and also the region as the water that is still there then you could expand the theory to see the ways it can enhance our lives through the proof that it really counts.

Now that you've gotten your head around the idea it is probably wondering where to look for itwhich is an additional challenge. As per Giorgi The "wherein" is much more an abstract location. "We are able to access it through watching the natural styles. The patterns reveal the inherent intelligence of nature. Similar to knowing that when autumn is over, winter follows. It's been recorded, patterns repeat. The psychics as well as fortune-tellers are masters at knowing the future; by detecting subtle patterns in our senate reality the intuition of a person develops into a finely tuned skill."

If you want to research your own soul's records, Giorgi says you can actually turn inward with the practice of meditation and exercise. She suggests observing patterns in your life as well as observing patterns that appear that are found in the natural world, as well as then the use of the information you have gathered to understand your own life. All of this is to suggest that everything is made up of something, and nothing can ever return to nothing Follow your gut and track your stepseven if you don't be able to see them.

Records of the Akashic Information

The akashic files were studied and referenced by the ancient Egyptians, Tibetans, Moors, Persians, Greeks, Jews, Druids, Indians and Mayans prior to reaching Western human consciousness. There are references to the hieroglyphs as well as historical texts However, the priests of the past were said to be the most literate to gain access to registers, whereas the most religious traditions stated that all and every one can have access to the file.

Akashic information, also known as "The Book of Life" For many, this book of existence is actually an picture of those who will go to heaven. Its origins lie in the tradition of recording information about genealogical relatives of names, or perhaps earlier census taking. The traditional belief suggests that this book, in its literal or symbolic form , contains the names of everyone who have merit to be saved. The book must be unveiled in relation to God's judgement (Dan. 7:10, Rev. 20:12). In 20:12 in the New Testament, those redeemed by Christ are included in the book (Philippians 4.). People who aren't found within the life-book won't be able to ascend into the realm of Heaven.

Blavatsky claimed to have done long hours of intense research with Tibetan clergymen. She referred to as the facts honestly "Akasha." Theosophy describes Akasha as the primary substance, which is the pressure that is essential. However, the it was most effective during the 20th century, early pioneers of metaphysical research such as Alice Bailey, Manley P. Corridor, Charles Leadbetter, and Annie Besant added the term Akashic information for the first period of.

Edgar Cayce additionally referred to as the prophet of drowsing, was the first to popularize the Akashic record idea through the Soul Readings. Cayce was raised within his Catholic Christian faith, and became a humble man. As an infant, Cayce was able to see spirits and other beings and his mother encouraged him to maintain his talents and abilities, which were a part of his life. He began to study his soul "with the help of a twist of fate" and, as a method to treat a persistent throat ache, he was taken into a realm of the hypnosis. Then it was discovered that it was possible to fall into a deep trance state that he could learn and help people.

Additionally, Cayce turned into channeling many fascinating information about the subject of astrology. He explained how astrology can be used to gather self-information. his belief changed to its goal was to gain spiritual growth by benefiting by gaining knowledge and guide our will to express our desires thoughts, hopes, and desires. He believed that astrology was an opportunity to realize that we're integral to the world around us in our solar systems. In 1936, while conducting an analysis of lifestyles for a woman of Canada, Cayce surely explained the goal of astrology in relation to our soul's enjoyment in "considering the existence of being a soul, an individual in a continuous stream of delight and actions on earth's surface as a lesson to be learned by the individual's experiences through the astrological time travels prove to be more of an assimilation or digesting of the knowledge that was achieved or acquired in the course." (Edgar Cayce analyzing 1230-1)

Cayce repeatedly stressed that we control the course of our lives by using our the free will of our own. One of the initial readings Cayce provided in connection with the astrological field on 1923. wrote: "...but let it be noted that there is no way that any movement of planets, phases of the solar system or lunar phases, the Moon or any of the heavenly bodies can override the rules of thumbs that man's will power, the power that is the creator of mankind, in the beginning, as the soul was made a living being and had the power of deciding for himself." (Edgar Cayce reading 3744-3) It is within this statement that Cayce gives us the outline of our lives If we choose to be conscious, we are aware of our relationship with the writer and, consequently, we learn our capacity to express of our creative talents and are able to.

Another fantastic call that is connected to the take a look at Akashic records is the one from Rudolph Steiner, that within the Gospel of Saint John stated"Everything that occurs within the body-feel-global has a equivalent in the non-secular. While a hand is moving and you look around, there is more than the hand moving by your eyes and that's my ideas and my desires"My hand has to move. Non-secular history exists. As the ocular, rational impact of the hand goes out it's non-secular counterpart stays imprinted in the non-secular universe and never fails to leave a footprint there. When our eyes open in the non-secular world and we can trace the tracks and discover the religious side of the entire thing that has happened across the world. There is nothing that can happen anywhere in the world without leaving these trace marks. Let's imagine the spiritual investigator , we could let be looking back at the time of Charlemagne or Roman periods, or even to the past of Greece.

Professor Ervin Laszlo, a renowned scientist, is among the top current students of Akashic statistics. He gave a fresh perspective that is based on research findings at the edge of physics that is decreasing. Instead of viewing the things we see as real, and the space in which they reside as a passive and empty space within the Akasha concept, he perceives the real space and the things contained within it are not the primary focus. In essence, he asserts that Akasha is a fusion of the old faith paradigms as well as the paradigms of modern science, giving insight into values such as real-world harmony and concord, as well as life-sustaining implications for humanity.

Edgar Cayce's works suggest that we all create the stories of our lives through our minds, our movements and interactions with the rest of the world. These numbers have an effect on us right now and right now. It is likely that there are numerous other things in our lives, our history, and that our own lives influence on us the world more than we've ever considered having. Being able to access the Akashic data can provide many of those figures. Do you want to take an examination?

Akashic records -- An Illuminating healing journey

I am able to recall the huge, tranquil area that was awash with the misty white light and pillars. I still feel the wonder from the first visit to this place when I was when I was a child. Whatever the authority within it this place was filled with an ethereal, soothing and loving energy. Everything looked bathed with sparkling, white light, as if the area was made of clouds. At the time, I could not fully comprehend the underlying meaning of what I was tapping into, however, I do know that the desire to remain there for longer.

I felt an unfathomable connection to this hidden area and was pleasantly surprised when I was able to access the Akashic information for the first time in the following years. The experience changed into one that was Deja vu, a feeling of returning home. When I opened my stats and listened to the soothing sounds of harp and chimes greeted me. A feeling of affection radiated from the data and I should feel the joy of love within my soul. In a state of affection, I saw images and words as if I were looking at the 4D version of a PowerPoint presentation.

Who're we?

Many people are seeking answers to the questions we have about our soul's journey in order to give the reason for our identity as well as what our soul's reason is, what be a part of it, and why certain things, issues, patterns and recurring issues are so prevalent within our daily lives? What makes no attempts sufficient to swap these patterns? It's as if you are caught in a circle in which all the elements (human beings, locations and even situations) trade, yet the patterns remain. They are just a matter of form and they don't go away.

We are divine in our essence. We are the essence of the source of all things, representing the highest level of love. We are a vital element of the public's attention and are not distant. Earth is our campus where we become human beings and live life after life. We review the guidelines to develop our souls through existence reviews in order to achieve the spiritual perfection we attain in the physical world. Through these reviews, we keep track of the non-secular journey and evolution, while retaining the subconscious desire to align with the ultimate purpose of our soul being one with the supply.

I think that during my initial conscious experience in the realm of Akashic statistics , I used to look for answers to a couple of issues. I didn't anticipate to gain the insight that came through the ages of not three lives prior. The fact that I used to be a victim of wonder is a bit of irony. I did not realize that the problems that affected one relationship would turn into a series of patterns manifesting in different areas of my life, and were no longer working for my favor. The root of the issues was sudden and it took a while before the realization to be absorbed. After recognizing the issue, I experienced a recovery by a feeling of release. Since the time that I began connecting to the potential of Akashic records I've been able of seeing past the illusionary and create choices that have led to (nonetheless opening) new possibilities and doors which I never dreamed of in the past.

What are Akashic Records?

Akasha is an Sanskrit word that is derived from the ether, which is first or primordial substance of which everything is created. It encompasses us in totality. Akashic records or the corridor of information as described by the various sources is an extensive library of light in which all the data and information pertaining to every soul who ever lived are encoded by light. The knowledge of Akashic details could be amazing and for many long periods of time, have been able for saints, seers and more developed souls. It's an obligation that is best left to those who are in a position to recognize the sacredness of it. However, in the Age of Aquarius, as humans are evolving and evolving, we've moved from a world of dependence to a society of responsibility, and we've taken the responsibility of our spiritual development and progress.

Akashic information has been around since the beginning of the time. In spite of the fact that the name originates from Sanskrit and is recognized and understood through unique names that span diverse religions and cultures (in the case of 'Torah', due to the book of remembrance, and in the Bible as a result of the ebook of life). In line to Garuda purana, Chitragupta records and compiles a record of every single action in every life form from the beginning to the death. In the mystical worldview, these documents are referred to as the Akashic information, believed to encompass every step that ever took place in the universe. Edgar Cayce (1877-1945), the yank mystic, also known as the "napping prophet" utilized the trance channeling method to gain access to the information and relayed figures and other information related to the human condition and spirituality. In addition to Edgar Cayce theosophist Helena Blavatsky (1831-1891) claimed, "indestructible capsules of the astral light" documenting the past as well as the future of human thought and movement;

Rudolf Steiner (1861-1925) also spoke of the Akashic information throughout his work. In line with the quantum scientist Ervin Laszlo - "its is the electromagnetic footprint of everything that occurs in the Universe." In simple terms, it would be true to say that Akashic records as a vibration-filing device where every emotion, thought, word and action that the soul produces of soul is awe-inspiring because it is recorded from the beginning and interprets it directly to transcendence, gift and the future.

What is the location of Akashic Records located, and how do they access them?

Akashic records are found in the higher state-conscious states of consciousness located in Akasha over the astral plane and are protected by the powerful spirits of the light. The gatekeepers of information have not been born. They no longer have physical names or bodies Their powerful energetic presence is only felt. Their responsibility is to ensure the integrity and sacredness of information is secured and preserved.

In addition to having access to records that go beyond lives, we can connect to the seventh vibration, and above which all details pertaining to beyond lifetimes are preserved. There are a variety of ways to being able to access the power that is the Akashic information such as meditation, trance channeling, prayers for sacred purposes, breathing strategies and so on. I make use of an oblation prayer to connect with the spirit and the soul truth. It is the key to quality music. It also provides the information and knowledge that are derived from this enchanting world. When the data is open, the Keepers of the data direct the way and, as they guide the data that is most valuable for the individual whom the data is being analyzed are pulled up.

In the sexy strength of the Akasha the inner sensory receptors awaken and the senses are heightened. When we are allow ourselves to be guided by Divine guidance and allow ourselves to access the profound knowledge that comes from the ascended gods of light.

What can the accessing of Akashic records aid in healing?

Looking for solutions We were looking for assistance from people who were seeking an ounce of light and a rationalization of the causes for the difficulties we're experiencing and the possibility of a brief recovery as a form of treatment. Although the electrical subject and vibrations can provide some data, the long-lasting healing power is within our soul.

When Akashic documents are available in a variety of ways, those that pertain to current life situations are typically identified. In general, latent forms are revealed so to be addressed. Akashic data is like an online resource (in case you think of it as they're actually an online library) The more questions we pose the more specific solutions we receive.

The specifics of the past lives like what I was in the world beyond or the things I did during my time in this life aren't necessarily essential. The most important thing is the wisdom that comes through having access to your lives, and the ability to see any karmic blocks, debts or patterns that may remain present through these life-styles as a result of past lives.

The research reveals the root cause of such types of karmic debts or blockages that generally can be traced back to earlier life experiences. Certain of them are linked to an unfinished venture or unfinished lessons that the soul needs to study. In a few instances they are triggers to keep the soul in mind of the lessons that it has learned from a previous lifetime that are ready to be activated by memories in this life.

The Akashic report Connection

It provides us with a sense of responsibility and deep healing as layers fall away, and we discover how we can transcend the illusion of space and time. Accessing the information from other people is an enriching experience as it's ideal to assist someone to progress along their path in life; but, often the information obtained contains wisdom that is applicable to our lives. One of the most common feedbacks I receive following an Akashic consults is "feeling light as if some weight has been taken off."

To get this and empowering tool, email us to find out more information about any of our forthcoming training workshops for certification near you.

"The records are in fact open."

My frame was more comfortable than when I had my back on my cushion for meditation.

The room mumbled the final line of The Pathway Prayer collectively a mantra to unlock the Akashic records, I sensed something change in my brain.

My body was weighed down to the ground. However, my head was a little sluggish it was as if the top of it had unfolded. It then changed to expand in parallel with every direction. I started to see flashes of pictures that I had by no ever seen before and then I began to hear words and phrases with a calmer and more pronounced rendition of the voice I had. In some way, I was aware that with every nerve of my body that the information I had discovered was not emanating from my mind ... regardless of the fact that the voice inside my head was saying, "perhaps you're making this up."

I didn't know the state I was entering into at the time of my initial meeting with the Akashic information. However I came away from the experience totally altered. It was like I had been given by the keys to in the Universe... And as someone who often (ahem frequently) discovers her mendacity-conscious around 3 a.M. In a state of anxiety about my future plans actually, was at calm.

"What is these Akashic Records?"

While you are listening to the word Akashic statistic, which thoughts come to your mind? When I first heard about it, my first thought turned into a vast collection of statistics. A lot of people think of the Akashic records as an ebook or library. Some people consider it to be an information database.

However, based on the data they could refer to an different dimension, known by the name of Akasha. This Akasha is a larger dimension than the one that we are living in.

Within the Akasha every thought or concept and every movements from past, present the future, and is stored in perpetuity. If you're familiar with the String idea it is the Akashic facts are in essence an archive of what's happening in all universes, which are co-current with each other.

The Akashic stats are in essence the record of what's coming to be revealed as it happens or is happening. Since they're a greater measure, the rules of time do not change in the way they are practiced. The circle of time is flat in the Akashic facts, which means that documents from 2,000 years ago are just as accessible as the records that was available to you in the previous day. And what happened in the past to you is just as possible as what will show before you if you are on the same direction within 10 years.

What experts say about the facts about akashic

Incredibly, everything has an individual Akashic record. Your soul is the Akashic report, your home is the Akashic document, and your dog even your courtship!

Here's the way Edgar Cayce, the psychic medium who popularized stats describe them:

It is believed that the Akashic statistics, also known as "The book of existence," can be equated to the universe's amazing computer gadget. This system is the primary repository of all the information available to anyone who has lived on earth. It is more than just a repository of historical events The Akashic records include every act and every word, thought of thought, intention, and thought that has occurred anytime in the history of the entire world. More than just storage of memory However, these Akashic records are interconnected because they have had an enormous impact on the way we live our lives and relationships, our beliefs and feelings as well as the possible possibilities we have drawn towards us ... They are the Akashic facts encompass the complete story of each soul's history due to the fact that the sun rises at the time of beginning. These facts link each of us with one another.

Linda Howe, the writer of the book that is extremely instructive, "how to study The Akashic statistics" describes them this way:

The Akashic information can help us achieve the possibility of transformation and empowerment by giving us the exact direction, guidance and active support that we require in this time. For centuries the information that was the active archive of Souls past, gifts and destiny possibilities been the exclusive realm of saints, mystics, and even students. No more! The focus of humanity is growing, changing and growing. This non-secular autonomy is reflected by those who acknowledge that they've gained access to their faith and cultivate this sacred relationship.

Chapter 11: How to Access Akashic Records

Accessing the getting access to the (or getting access to the corridor (or Library) access to the corridor (or Library) Akashic Records isn't difficult. It's not something that's given to just the handful of people who have it but the Universe does not make distinctions. There are a variety of ways to gain access to. Be careful not to get caught up in the practice of astral projection, or any of the other methods. Simply because you are studying someone who has that has accessed the Akashic record in this manner. It's like thinking that you should practice skateboarding since you study the person who was given to the library by the public on skateboard. Choose the best skateboard you are a fan of skateboarding to ensure that it gets access to the Akashic records. Choose the one that is easy and effective for you.

The motivation is more important than the ability. If someone tries to go into the realm of the Akashic facts simply out of curiosity, and not declare malicious motives the chances are they'll be rejected or confused. It could sound innocent enough, like "allow's know what my boyfriend/girlfriend has is like in their past lives." But ..." learning who they were , but it won't help your relationship until you know what you're about. It is always necessary to know to know.

That's the main advantage of studying Akashic data: to recognize the person you are. We like to believe that we know ourselves but the truth is that we don't. Psychologists explain this using Johari window. Johari window. Also, the portion of you that isn't aware of could affect you and your decisions.

Here is a simple yet efficient method of studying the Akashic data.

A study of the psychic isn't something more than a well-developed ability. The book was not designed to focus on improving your psychic ability However, anyone who is interested can read it. this is a guide to studying your personal Akashic data. Use it to increase your knowledge of your own personal development.

Examining your personal Akashic information isn't a requirement to be granted access to the corridor of Akashic records, where all Akashic data is kept. The Akashic records are active copies of your personal Akashic records. Therefore, analyzing your personal Akashic data is not too difficult; however there are a few conditions. One of them is the ability to enter the state of meditative nations. While the normal intuition may be triggered in a non-sensical manner, studying the Akashic stats requires more focus. You must have a goal to distinguish your current thinking and be open to any stats you find.

The other requirement is the acceptance and willingness to share things that are recorded regarding you. It is possible that you will be confronted with alarming facts, like the manner in which you died in one of your past life experiences or some serious problems that plagued your life for a long time earlier in your life and how you played a role in the issue. If, in the course of your everyday routine, you are inclined to avoid trouble or avoid difficult situations, how do you deal with such information when you are reading your Akashic data?

Although it's not necessarily a requirement, having a compassionate understanding of humankind and its history can be helpful to make the study useful. For instance, let's imagine that you discover you've been a slave driver until you're not worthy of life. If you think that's a terrible thing to be close to your heart, the analysis is over. Being a slave-driving power, it doesn't necessarily mean you were a cruel and cruel person or woman. Perhaps you were able to treat them as gently and as fair as possible however, since you've been in the middle management and not the owner and the sole proprietor, there was not a much you could do. This catch 22 scenario is the reason you're hesitant to accept the new managerial position. You are scared of being in the same kind of situation. A review can be as thorough as the depth of your knowledge about existence.

In order to begin the analysis of your Akashic information, you'd likely want to perform certain ritual. A premeditative meditation is a good idea. Making your goal clear is an incredible exercise. You can say something like "let the force of love light, reality, and light succeed on this planet. My guides from spirit will assist me to open my Akashic records to ensure that I gain the wisdom to live my life with more awareness and courage." This "Love mild, gentle and truth" aspect is crucial. It is clear that you're studying with love, not making judgments, and with light (religious consciousness) and not in confusion, and to be honest instead of burying yourself in a lie or lack of details. In various ways it is a signal that you're open to the reality that something could be, and you're disposed to take it in with light and love.

I no longer suggest to read the Akashic information with just interest, as it can the ability to be extremely effective. If you simply think, "What became I doing in my previous life?" you could obtain information about all of your prior lives, no matter how significant that life's experience might be to your present life. The answers could be vague and elusive. As with many intuitive questions asking for the Akashic information should be simple and clear. Therefore, please take the time to take the time to read the Akashic records to help you fix the issue. For instance, you might wish to ask, "This (short description of your problem) is the issue I've been battling with and I feel that there's something else than I can see in my current life. If this is true then please provide the information of the time and date and how the issue began."

It is possible to see a picture or video clip that will catch your active attention. You could listen to music that evokes something. It could be that you feel it, smell it or even taste it. It is possible that you have it in your mind.

Perhaps it could be the sum of several of these. Get the data and ask any additional questions, if needed follow up, and end the discussion with a smile. You will get access to the amount of data as is useful to you currently.

How can you tell if you've obtained the correct information? It will be awe-inspiring and sense to you. It's possible to even experience changes. While this isn't the case with each precise analysis I've heard of some thrilling incidents such as pains disappearing or relationships growing or ending with no reason. Some people also temporarily feel low, along with feeling cold before feeling better.

There are certain instances when the right analysis doesn't resonate to you. In reality you'd be tempted dismiss the study using any method. This is when you're studying popular shows that reveal the most unpleasant information about you. If this is the case, it's an excellent option to stop moving back to denial. The discomfort of this study could be the first step towards changing your life if you decide to choose.

Additional cautions Particularly in the beginning, try to keep your consults brief. The Akashic information is a staggering amount of data, so it is essential to pay concentration. In other words you may be overwhelmed by the sheer volume of various pieces of information. This could lead to inaccuracy while reading. In the meantime, your brain can be overwhelmed. Don't be enticed by your curiosity.

When we're talking about the Akashic information, I would like to warn you not to study other people's Akashic data unless you've received their permission in writing. We make available the data and information contained in the Akashic information, however, it doesn't mean you have the right to invade the privacy of others. The study of Akashic stats is like entering a house and taking a look around. If it's your home you are entitled to conduct this. You are the owner of items you've put away so that you are able to access the containers and examine the contents. In other homes However, you shouldn't simply walk in and look about. Even if you intend to be charitable, it's not your responsibility to make that happen. One exception is the ones who have a significant impact on your life, such as your family members. You can look up their Akashic data in the amount that is pertinent to you.

Anyone who tries to get into the Akashic records may also be able to acquire incorrect statistics. They may be able to make statements which sound like they are and may appear to be accurate, but aren't necessarily true. This is the reason why a handful of books about or about the Akashic data or the beyond-existence regression seem too complicated. They're weaving unreliable and inaccurate statistics together.

These Akashic data are our collective help throughout the evolution of this universe. It is possible that at the time this universe is over or a different one begins with another huge Bang and we'll be able to access any of Akashic information. In the meantime, please view this report as a positive one.

Accessing Akashic records

In theosophy and anthroposophy the akashic truths (from the word "akasha," which is the Sanskrit word meaning "sky," "area," or "aether") are a collection of mystical wisdom that is encoded in a non-body-space of existence, referred to by the name of astral. The Akashic records contain every thought that has ever existed and every possibility that has ever been in an attempt to become. You can discover more about your past lives having access to your own Akashic records, and it could help you understand yourself on a spiritual level. While it's possible to take time and effort to find the information you're looking for and you'll have the capability of getting access to your Akashic records by using a basic method of meditation.

The focus you're seeking

Make yourself aware of your motives in order to gain access to the Akashic information

Before you decide to apply for access into Akashic records, before you attempt to gain access Akashic records, you'll need to consider the reason you're required to complete the process. What is it that you should know and how can this knowledge help you? Be clear about this before you begin.

It could be that your intentions are based on knowing the reason you are prone to a temper flare to help you understand how to manage it more effectively, getting clear about your goals so that you can make an important career choice, or becoming aligned with your beliefs so that you are seeking similar-minded people to form relationships with.

Tips Make sure you take your time in finding what you're looking for in the Akashic data.

The more specific you are with your question, the more successful the outcome you will get. You can try loose writing, talking with your friends, and studying to identify your motives for accessibility to Akashic records.

For instance you could ask "What occupations did I hold in my past life?" or "where did I reside in my past life?" or "Have I ever been through a tragic event in my beyond life that have a direct impact on my current life?"

Ask questions to aid you in deciding on your current life. Discuss a issue that you've experienced and then ask the country or for the information you'd prefer to have. This can help narrow your search and make information you discover more relevant to your current enjoyment.

Or, "these days I've been struggling to believe that I am distinct. I believe that this is due to something more than what I know about in my own life. If you believe me Please provide me with facts about when and where this issue started."

You can ask one question at a time , to gain an understanding more

This method could help improve the readability of troublesome issues like you might be able to focus on one aspect of your life at a time while using the use of a tarot deck or hand-reading. Concentrate on your work, relationships or health, as well as other hobbies in succession.

If you are still unsure, be asking, "Will I get the promotion I've been working to achieve or do I need to hold off?"

Coming into a Receptive country

Make sure you state your intent or ask a question in public and ask for direction.

If you feel ready to start the process of getting access to your Akashic facts, talk about what you're searching for loudly. Keep your attention on the issue or search query you've mastered. Keep it in the top of your list so that you remain focused on it throughout your research.

Keep in mind for the world that your query is especially feasible, such as declaring, "What professions did I have in my previous lives that might assist me in discovering what I need to be in the present?"

Sit or lay down in a tranquil, calm area

It is possible to access your Akashic archives anywhere. However it will allow you to access them in the event you're in a place where you might be interrupted. Make sure to access this within your bedroom with the doors shut. It is possible to perform this in the early morning or at night or during the afternoon when nobody else is home. Make use of blankets and pillows to relax.

Take a deep breath for five minutes or more to ease your mind.

Begin by closing your eyes while taking several deep breaths. Inhale with your nose until the number four and then hold for four seconds and exhale with your mouth until the number of 4. Keep breathing deeply in this manner for 5 minutes or however long you need to be to a deep state of relaxation.

Make sure to put your hands on your stomach to increase your breathing awareness.

Take a moment to think about your question when you're at peace and in a calm and relaxed.

Once you've in a state of total relaxation, let go from all thoughts, excluding your question. Make sure to repeat your question or ask a question like an ode to the living center. Your mind might also be fumbling in a few instances or even thoughts that aren't normal. If you say something and your thoughts wander to daily worries, keep yourself to your mantra and continue to meditate. Take deep breaths throughout the meditation.

You can request to be granted access into the Akashic records

After you've meditated for five minutes or more it is possible of accessing the Akashic documents. Also, can I go to the Akashic data to determine the information I'm looking for?" after you ask the question, make sure to breathe deeply and clear your mind.

You might observe, feel the sensation, or observe a reaction in your mind's eye. Be patient, even when you have an unsatisfactory response. This could mean that you keep your focus and keep asking.

TIP: Be aware that for a small percentage of people, accessing the Akashic information requires several tries. If it's not perfect the first timearound, do not be discouraged! Keep trying until you find the information you're looking for.

Watch for data to be uncovered

Once you've put your request and question to gain the right to enter the Akashic record to space and time, the only thing to do is just sit. Remain in a state of meditation and breathing, being open to any information that comes in your awareness, since this might be coming from the records of your Akashic record.

Be aware that facts could be a source of extraordinary bureaucracy. You might be paying attention, observe or feel, or smell something intended to communicate some message to you.

For instance, if you've been asked about your work in a past life and you can observe a hammer in your vision, which could suggest that you've been a blacksmith or carpenter. You might also have a sweet taste which might indicate that you've been baking.

Be aware that you could receive information regarding your past experiences in the past that could be disturbing. However, it is essential to be open to the details and not judge yourself for any untrue behavior to benefit the most out of your Akashic analysis.

Introduce yourself and reiterate your question to every person you come to

Every now and then during your time of accessing the Akashic archives, you might perhaps feel or see the presence of any other being or soul that's close to. If this occurs then introduce yourself and ask the question again. It could be a mother or father or someone who is the keeper of the information that lets you discover the information you're looking for It could also be an individual you've had a relationship with in your past. Whatever the case, you may gain valuable information through making a point introduction and asking for assistance.

Try saying something like "Hey My name is Jonah Johnson, and I'm seeking records of my phobias in my other lives."

How to decipher what you find

Take a step back and open your eyes to reorient yourself towards the world around you

When you've had access to your data or at any time you're prepared to end the practice, gradually open your eyes. Pay attention to the details of the space you're in as well as the sound of the room, the smells, and the textures of your surroundings. Recover slowly as if you were lying down. You may also stand up or remain sitting for a few minutes in the event that you would like.

Revel in the moment the end of your meditation

What photos did you see? Did you feel a lingering smell or taste? Did you be aware of any other aspect? Examine your notes to find important information from your meditation. You should also keep your notes to return to them later.

Tips: Be aware that some of the information you get at some point during the course of your visit won't be believable or seem relevant. But, by keeping pursuing access to the Akashic documents, you will understand the significance of these images becomes more clear and more clear.

Repeat the process often to learn more

Set a timer at least once a week to practice this meditation and gain access to the Akashic documents. You can keep the same questions each time or think of another question when you are satisfied with the outcome from your final session.

In the event that you are confident that you've acquired knowledge about all of your other professional activities, you can immediately ask about your relationships beyond them next.

Are we able to obtain the right to enter our Akashic information?

Is the Akashic statistics only a small collection of cosmic reports on shelves in endless aisles and stacks? What is the context from which this notion originate? Are these records present in space and time like a galactic network? What are the steps to gain access in these records? Akashic records?

While many may describe or offer an explanation of the idea in specific ways In fundamental terms it is it is the Akashic data are considered to be the source of all thoughts, words and action of every living being, good terrible, horrible, and right at all times and beyond the present the present, and destiny. However, those who have studied the data know that there's no judgement or implied punishment in the facts they're said to be an accurate record of the journey of every soul's soul across the vast.

History of the Akashic Records

Akashic data is now compiled by Helena Blavatsky, founding father of the Theosophical movement in the latter half of the 19th century. Blavatsky claimed that she learned the information from Tibetan monks. They claimed that the data was in"akasha," or "akasha," or "ether," a connection with the distance element found in jap five-element patterns. The 5th element of space is regarded as the core of truth from which the other elements arise as the source of the material truth.

The metaphysician Rudolf Steiner also referenced the Akashic statistics, saying that every word, movement or concept creates a trace in the states of the ether. Modern scientist Ervin Laszlo examines the values of Akasha in relation to the mindset of technology and concludes that Akasha provides a template that human beings can use, like peace and harmony. The concept is explored on in the "Akasha Paradigm" which he connects to the evolutionary techniques of humans.

Participants in Akashic document styles frequently reference Scripture as the "ebook that records life" which was first mentioned in the old testament (Exodus). Scripture affirms that a written record of each life is kept at the top of heaven. It's from the statistics by which souls are assessed.

Who is able to be able to read those Akashic records?

While Debbie Ritter may additionally dispute the "expert" attribute and is not an expert, she's qualified. After having studied Mandarin Chinese language, practicing environmental regulation, and continuing study of shamanism, yoga, Buddhism, and a path to Miracles and a path to acquire local intuitional skills. Through a variety of teachers, she learned about Akashic data with author Linda Howe. She is now an intuitive teacher of existence psychic medium, psychic medium, as well as an Akashic Data Reader.

In response to questions about barriers in accessing the information, she stated that the device is, actually, not everyone's "aspect." The researcher said, "Running in the statistics could be something some individuals are interested in but for others, there is nothing that clicks. If this happens it's valid to find another option or method to ensure that it resonates with the individual. I've seen this happen when I'm conducting brief intros. In the interest of their private curiosity that they can move to another topic."

She explained that a different obstacle is disbelief. She explained that many are fighting against prejudices or are unsure of their own belief. Whatever the case, Ritter believes no person can be secluded from facts. "It's but not something I experience as an instructor or reader," she said, saying that some people stay away from the facts due to tension. "It's distances as the individual to decide whether to keep or not. In my instance it was clear that my internal issues were getting agitated. I was able to get an understanding from all the sources and also make small internal adjustments."

"Similarly there isn't any "future" or "fate" within the data, because its existence is the result an array of ever-changing interactions and synergies. Life is more complicated than the world, and there might be no reality in the world outside," she stated.

Methods to gain access to the Akashic records

The search term "get access into Akashic archives" on Amazon currently yields 14 pages of results Google provides 416,000 results. A plethora of YouTube authorities are asking for "the method to gain access to Akashic data" information, conjunction with hypnosis products that claim to lead listeners directly into the halls of cosmic majesty.

The people who have access to the information report that patrons can also enjoy meeting books angels, astrologers, and the background of the scenes players. It is evident that the galactic library is well-staffed. Some claim that accessing statistics is a kind of "channeling" while others claim that they access data through desire.